Praise for *So, You Want to Start a Business?*

"I used *So, You Want To Start a Business?* to restructure my furniture hardware company. The book was full of applicable information that I have used and will continue to incorporate into my company. I couldn't ask for a better resource."

—Adam Prestwood, Vice President,
Pampco, Inc.

"Practical, sensible advice to anyone starting a business. A great short course in entrepreneurship."

—Billy D. Prim, Chairman and CEO,
Primo Water Corporation, Winston-Salem, NC

"This is exactly the kind of book first time entrepreneurs always needed but was never available. Everyone who is thinking about becoming an entrepreneur must read this book."

—Dr. E.W. Leonard, Associate Dean, Executive MBA Program,
Goizueta Business School, Emory University

"Here is the straight story about being a successful entrepreneur from people who have been one and taught many. Clear, practical, and concise, this book delivers the goods."

—Andy Fleming, Principal,
Core Growth Partners, Atlanta, GA

"Solid advice for building and growing a sustainable business."

—Andrew Bourne, CEO,
WayPoint Technologies, Phoenix, AZ

"Professor Hess's book has helped me improve my services and make clients feel appreciated, respected, and most of all, like they're getting a great service at a fair price."

—Sammy Starnes, Owner,
Hair Concepts, Inc.

"A treasure trove of information! I just started my company, and I have to say that this book helped me make the right decisions from the very beginning."

—Derica Justice, Owner,
Bon Bini Print & Design

D1005421

"This is a great practical guide with lessons and insights for anyone who wants to start a business. You will go back to it again and again."

Ned Morgens, CEO,
SarahCare.com, Atlanta, GA

"Whether you are a striving young entrepreneur or a middle-aged person with the courage to trust your wits, this book is indispensable."

—Ben Dyer, General Partner,
Cordova Ventures, Atlanta, GA

"A must read for entrepreneurs who want to know what it really takes to launch a successful small business."

—Jay Myers, CEO,
Interactive Solutions, Inc., Memphis, TN

"A precise, pragmatic, wisdom-dripping, rich read. The authors walk the talk."

—Jim Christian, CEO,
Kandumedia.com, Denver, CO

"A powerful book full of good how-to advice."

—Philippe Sommer, Director of Entrepreneurship Programs,
Batten Institute, Darden School of Business, Charlottesville, VA

"This book is a great primer and an excellent reference book for an entrepreneur."

—Walter Negley, CEO,
TSP, Houston, TX

So, YOU
WANT TO START A
BUSINESS?

So, **YOU** WANT TO START A **BUSINESS?**

8 STEPS TO TAKE BEFORE MAKING THE LEAP

EDWARD D. HESS AND CHARLES F. GOETZ

Vice President, Publisher: Tim Moore
Associate Publisher and Director of Marketing: Amy Neidlinger
Acquisitions Editor: Jennifer Simon
Editorial Assistant: Pamela Boland
Development Editor: Russ Hall
Operations Manager: Gina Kanouse
Digital Marketing Manager: Julie Phifer
Publicity Manager: Laura Czaja
Assistant Marketing Manager: Megan Colvin
Marketing Assistant: Brandon Smith
Cover Designer: Chuti Prasertsith
Managing Editor: Kristy Hart
Project Editor: Anne Goebel
Copy Editor: Language Logistics
Proofreader: Kathy Ruiz
Senior Indexer: Cheryl Lenser
Senior Compositor: Gloria Schurick
Manufacturing Buyer: Dan Uhrig

Library of Congress Cataloging-in-Publication Data

Hess, Edward D.

So, you want to start a business? : 8 steps to take before making the leap / Edward D. Hess, Charles F. Goetz.

p. cm.

Includes bibliographical references.

ISBN 0-13-712667-0 (pbk. : alk. paper) 1. New business enterprises. 2. Entrepreneurship.
3. Business planning. I. Goetz, Charles F., 1956- II. Title.

HD62.5.H475 2009

658.1'1—dc22

2008014682

To all the entrepreneurs who have taught me that business is
much more than just making money;
it is the primary means through which most people achieve
their dreams for a better life for themselves and their families.
To that end business is a noble profession.
—Ed Hess

I dedicate this book to everyone who dreams of a better life and who is will-
ing to accept some risk so that they can see their dreams come true.
And to my family, who has made it possible for me to achieve my dreams.
Thank you—I love you all.
—Charlie Goetz

Contents

Acknowledgments xvii

About the Authors xix

Introduction xx
Who Should Buy This Book? xx
Why Is This Book Important? xx
What Topics Are Covered? xx
Why Are We Qualified to Write This Book? xxi
How to Use This Book xxii

Chapter 1   Can You Be a Successful Entrepreneur? 1
What Do Successful Entrepreneurs Do? 2
Who Are Successful Entrepreneurs? 3
    Key Definitions 5
Two Common Paths to Entrepreneurial
Success 5
Chapter One: Lessons Learned 6

Chapter 2   Basic Rules of Business Success 9
The 8 Common Start-Up Mistakes 10
    Common Mistake #1: Choosing a Bad
    Business Opportunity 10
    Common Mistake #2: Choosing the
    Wrong Customers 12
    Common Mistake #3: The Wrong Product 12
    Common Mistake #4: Pricing Products
    or Services Improperly 13

Common Mistake #5: Not Selling to Enough Customers Fast Enough 14

Common Mistake #6: Not Executing Well 15

Common Mistake #7: People Problems 16

Common Mistake #8: Mismanaging Growth 17

Basic Rules of Business Success 18

Chapter Two: Lessons Learned 19

Chapter 3   **What Is a Good Business Opportunity?** 21

Pencil It 23

Example 1: The Best Sandwich Shop 24

What Is the Average Price You Can Sell Your Sandwiches For? 25

Competitors 26

Back to the Math 28

Example 2: Children's Clothing Shop 30

Customer Conversion Ratio 31

Customer Conversion Rates 32

Two Different Types of Businesses 32

Estimating Your Costs 35

What Does Net Profit Margin Tell You About Costs? 36

Why Do You Need to Know Your Costs? 37

7 Ws 38

Chapter Three: Lessons Learned 38

Chapter 4   **How Do You Choose the Right Customers?** ... 41

The Right Customers 42

Who Is a Prospect? *42*

Example Survey Questions *47*

The Competition 52

Chapter Four: Lessons Learned 58

Chapter 5   **How Do You Design Your Product
or Service?** 59

Give Customers Only What They
Truly Need 60

Features or Benefits 60

What Is Value? 61

Example: Enhancing Your Product/Service
Value 62

Your "Reason for Being" 66

Low Innovation 68

It's Now Time to Build Your Product/Service ... 69

Can You Build or Produce It? 70

The Prototype—The Test 70

*What Is a Prototype and How Does
It Work?* *71*

Other Tips *71*

3 Ws *74*

Chapter Five: Lessons Learned 74

Chapter 6　What Is the Right Price for Your Product
or Service? 77

　　　　　Competitive Pricing 80

　　　　　Break-even Formula 81

　　　　　　*Number of Products Required to Be
　　　　　　Sold to Break Even* 82

　　　　　Additional Pricing Factors 82

　　　　　Chapter Six: Lessons Learned 84

Chapter 7　How Can You Overcome Customer Inertia? . . . 87

　　　　　Obstacles to a Sale 88

　　　　　The Risks of Buying from You 89

　　　　　Making Sales Takes Practice 92

　　　　　　The Psychology of Sales 92

　　　　　　The Customer Buying Timeline 92

　　　　　　*Time Is Your Enemy—Your Money
　　　　　　Is Burning* 93

　　　　　　Selling Is Like Fishing 93

　　　　　　*Customer Referral Programs and
　　　　　　Customer Loyalty Programs* 94

　　　　　　Start with a Customer 94

　　　　　Chapter Seven: Lessons Learned 95

Chapter 8　How to Manage Your Business 97

　　　　　Start-Up Overload 98

　　　　　Your Value Chain 99

　　　　　Your Supply Chain 100

　　　　　Your Manufacturing (Assembling) Chain 101

　　　　　Why Do You Flow Chart Your Business? 102

Management by Objectives 103

Management by Exceptions 106

The Power of Simplicity 108

    Rule of 3s *109*

    Rule of 7s *110*

Measurements and Rewards 110

Stay on the Front Lines 114

Iteration 114

Make Work Fun 115

Chapter Eight: Lessons Learned 116

Chapter 9   **How Do You Find and Keep Good
Employees?** 119

This People Stuff Is Hard 120

What Do Employees Want? 121

Why Is High Employee Turnover Bad? 121

Hire for Fit 121

Hiring Tools 122

    Probationary Hiring *123*

Buy-In 123

The Rules of the Game 124

Best Practices of Managing Employees 124

    Promote from Within *125*

    The Meaning of Work *126*

Mental Rehearsal 127

Mental Replay 127

Chapter Nine: Lessons Learned 128

Chapter 10 **How Do You Manage Growth?** 131

Growth Can Be Good or Bad 132

The Two Absolutes 134

Process 135

Financing Growth 136

Financial Controls 137

Managing the Unexpected 137

People 138

Small Business Services 139

Check-Off 140

Legal 140

Legal Structure 140

Small Business Networks 141

Upgrading People 142

Customer Diversification 142

Growth Changes Your Job 142

Chapter Ten: Lessons Learned 145

Conclusion 147

Business Rules 148

Lessons Learned 160

Bibliography and Resources 169

Books 169

"Building a Company" Books *169*

Business Strategy Books *172*

Entrepreneurship Books *173*

CONTENTS

Family Business Books *174*

*Finance, Accounting, and Measurement
    Books* *175*

Leadership Books *176*

*Books on Lessons to Learn from Bad
    Leadership* *178*

Management Books *178*

Marketing and Sales Books *180*

Articles 181

Information Portals 183

Author's Commentaries 184

Index 187

Acknowledgments

No one writes a book by himself. This book is the result of over 30 years of learning from teachers, entrepreneurs, colleagues, and students too numerous to mention by name—but thank you.

A special thank you to Deans Al Hartgraves and Tom Robertson who gave me the opportunity to create the Entrepreneurship and Entrepreneurial Leadership courses at the Goizueta Business School at Emory University.

Thank you to consummate entrepreneurs Ben Dyer and Jay Myers who graciously critiqued the book.

To Dean Bob Bruner and Professor Jeanne Liedtka, Executive Director of the Batten Institute, at the Darden School of Business, and the Darden Foundation, at the University of Virginia—thank you for your support in this endeavor and for the privilege to be a faculty member at Darden.

And to my dear friend, colleague, and coauthor Charlie Goetz who epitomizes the American dream—thank you for your contribution and for the joy and fun of trying to help others achieve their dreams. You are a good soul.

Thank you to my Executive Assistant, Nanci Crawford, who makes writing more of a joy with her high standards and management of the book production process.

And a special thanks to the wonderful team at Pearson (led by our editor Jen Simon, who believed in this project as passionately as we did) who made our book better and were great partners with positive entrepreneurial attitudes.

—Ed Hess

First off, I would like to apologize for those who I might have inadvertently left out. If your name is not on this list and it should have been, unfortunately you are one of them—my sincere apology.

There have been many people who have directly and indirectly helped me in the writing of this book. In many cases, they don't even know they helped, including some of my colleagues and students at Emory and the entrepreneurs and board members that I work closely with every day.

That said, I want to thank Mike Parham, Eric Hartz, David Zalik, Adam Leaderman, Randall Bentley, Byron Kopman, and Harold Enoch.

Most importantly, though, I want to give special thanks to Ed Hess. To his credit, he recognized before anyone else that there is a large market of want-to-be entrepreneurs who have had little business training and that they deserved a tool of their very own they could use to achieve the type of business success they too have been dreaming of.

So, You Want to Start a Business? was his dream and a worthy endeavor. I very much appreciate that he allowed me to come along.
—**Charlie Goetz**

About the Authors

Edward D. Hess is a Professor of Business Administration and Batten Executive-in-Residence at the Darden School of Business at the University of Virginia. Prior to joining Darden, he was Adjunct Professor of Business, Founder and Executive Director of both the Center for Entrepreneurship & Corporate Growth and the Values-Based Leadership Institute at the Goizueta Business School, Emory University.

Professor Hess is the author/editor of five other books and over 40 articles on business strategy, finance, growth, and family businesses. He is a magna cum laude graduate of the University of Florida and received a J.D. degree from the University of Virginia and an LL.M degree from New York University.

He is a frequent speaker, and his work has appeared in the *Financial Times*, *Fortune* magazine, and on CNBC.

Prior to joining academia, Professor Hess spent 30 years in the business world as a lawyer, investment banker, strategy consultant, and entrepreneur with Atlantic Richfield Company, Warburg Paribas Becker, Boettcher & Company, The Robert M. Bass Group, and Andersen Corporate Finance. His primary business focus has been private entrepreneurial businesses, and he has built three successful service businesses. He has taught courses on Entrepreneurship, Entrepreneurial Leadership, Organic Growth, and Managing Small Businesses. His writings and books can be found at www.EDHLTD.com.

Charles F. Goetz is the Distinguished Lecturer in Entrepreneurship at the Goizueta Business School at Emory University. Prior to joining Emory, Mr. Goetz was a successful serial entrepreneur. He built nine businesses, which in total employed over 1,500 people. He was successful in selling a number of these businesses while also experiencing some failures. Combined, these businesses gave him a valuable insight into understanding what it truly takes to build a successful business.

Professor Goetz serves on the Boards of Directors of several entrepreneurial venture and not-for-profit organizations. He is also an Angel investor in several businesses and is a frequent speaker on Entrepreneurship and Business Development. He recently published his first book, *The Great Entrepreneurial Divide: The Winning Tactics of Successful Entrepreneurs and Why Everyone Else Fails!* In addition, he has been recognized by Emory students as an Outstanding Lecturer in the MBA and Executive MBA Programs. Prior to becoming an entrepreneur, Professor Goetz was a senior executive at Citicorp. He has a BA in Economics from Emory University and an MBA from the University of Texas at Austin.

Introduction

Welcome to our book! In this introduction, we want to answer a few questions that many of you may have:

- Should you buy this book?
- Why is this book important?
- What topics are covered?
- Why are the authors qualified to write this book?

Who Should Buy This Book?

This book was written to help anyone starting a business—whether he or she is a business person or not. This book also should be helpful for anyone who has started a business and is not making enough money. Lastly, this book should help anyone investing in a start-up because most start-ups face the same challenges.

Why Is This Book Important?

Over 5,000,000 new businesses are started each year, but millions will fail, and most new businesses fail for the same sets of reasons. Our experience has taught us that there are 8 common reasons why start-ups fail, and with our combined 50 years building, financing, and teaching others how to build successful businesses behind us, in this book we offer ways to avoid making those 8 common mistakes.

What Topics Are Covered?

Our goal is simple and focused: to teach you how to avoid the 8 common mistakes many start-ups make.

Ask ten people why so many new business ventures fail, and many will answer, "Because the new business was undercapitalized." Undercapitalized means the business runs out of money before it makes enough profit to survive. We disagree with that conclusion. Running out of money is the result or consequence of more fundamental, underlying failures—the 8 common mistakes—which we teach you how to avoid.

People run out of money because they make one or more of the following 8 common mistakes:

1. Choosing a bad business opportunity (Chapter 3)
2. Choosing the wrong customers (Chapter 4)
3. Trying to sell the wrong product (Chapter 5)
4. Selling for the wrong price (Chapter 6)
5. Overestimating the number of and the speed of customer purchases (Chapter 7)
6. Mismanaging the business (Chapter 8)
7. Failing to hire and retain the right people (Chapter 9)
8. Being unable to grow or scale the business to accommodate growth (Chapter 10)

This book will direct your focus to the 3 Ws:

1. **W**hat will you sell?
2. **W**ho will buy?
3. **W**hy will they buy?

Why Are We Qualified to Write This Book?

Ed Hess lives in Charlottesville, Virginia, and spent most of his business life advising entrepreneurs and financing their business ventures. He went to college at the University of Florida and to law school at the University of Virginia and graduate law school at New York University. Ed's professional career was spent with firms like Atlantic Richfield Company, Warburg Paribus Becker, Boettcher and Company, The Robert M. Bass Group, and Andersen Corporate Finance, and he has built three service businesses.

In 1999, Ed began teaching business students part-time at Goizueta Business School, Emory University, during which time he created and taught the entrepreneurship course. In 2002, Ed joined the faculty at Goizueta full-time as an Adjunct Professor where he became the Founder and Executive Director of both the Center for Entrepreneurship and Corporate Growth and the Values-Based Leadership Institute.

Ed has written five other books:

- Hess, Edward D. *Make It Happen! 6 Tools for Success* (EDHLTD, 2001).
- Hess, Edward. *The Successful Family Business: Proactively Managing Both the Family and the Business* (Praeger: Westport, Connecticut, 2005).
- Hess and Kazanjian, eds. *The Search for Organic Growth* (Cambridge University Press: New York, 2006).
- Hess and Cameron, eds. *Leading with Values: Positivity, Virtue and High Performance* (Cambridge University Press: New York, 2006).
- Hess, Edward. *The Road to Organic Growth: How Great Companies Consistently Grow Marketshare from Within* (McGraw-Hill: New York, 2007).

In July 2007, Ed joined the Faculty of the Darden School of Business at the University of Virginia as a Professor of Business Administration and Batten Executive-in-Residence where he teaches courses on building small businesses and organic growth.

Charlie Goetz earned his college degree at Emory University and holds an MBA from the University of Texas. Charlie is a successful serial entrepreneur. He built several successful businesses, which in total employed over 1,500 people. He sold most of his businesses and made substantial amounts of money their sales. Charlie then began teaching entrepreneurship at Emory University in the Goizueta Business School where he was again successful. His courses are always oversubscribed, and he has earned multiple teaching awards.

Today, Charlie lives in Atlanta, Georgia, and is an investor in several new businesses and consults with people starting businesses. His specialties are marketing, customer acquisition, and product development.

How to Use This Book

There are two ways to use this book:
1. Read it from start to finish. It was written in a specific order—tracing a business idea from the idea stage through the steps of building a business.

2. If you want to focus on a specific question, issue, or problem, go to that chapter. Each chapter will stand by itself.

This book will not guarantee that you will be successful, but it should help you avoid the 8 common mistakes made by start-up businesses.

Can You Be a Successful Entrepreneur?

CHAPTER TOPICS

- *What do successful entrepreneurs do?*
- *Who are successful entrepreneurs?*
- *Two common paths to entrepreneurial success*

You have decided to open a business. Now what? What product or service do you want to sell? Who needs that product or service? As you explore the pages that follow, you must consider every aspect of what you need to know to succeed and avoid the common pitfalls.

> **Business Rule #1:**
> The Jerry McGuire Rule:
> Follow the Money—Cash is King.

What Do Successful Entrepreneurs Do?

Successful entrepreneurs satisfy
CUSTOMERS' NEEDS
better, faster, and/or cheaper
than someone else (the competition).

Business is a game—a serious game. It is a competition. You keep score by adding up sales (cash received from customers), and you make sales by meeting or satisfying customer needs.

> **Business Rule #2:**
> The Peter Drucker Rule:
> "The sole purpose of business is to serve customers."

Peter Drucker was one of the leading business management thinkers of the last decade. He understood that every business is a service business regardless of what product it sells because the primary purpose of a business is to serve customers. To serve customers you must satisfy their needs at a better price or with better service than your competition does.

Who Are Successful Entrepreneurs?

Many people think that to be a successful entrepreneur, you need to be smart, have money, have a college degree, be an inventor, do something which never has been done before, and/or be willing to risk all your savings and your family's money.

Wrong, Wrong, Wrong, WRONG

To be a successful entrepreneur:

---

*You do **NOT** have to be an "A" student.*

*You do **NOT** have to have a college degree.*

*You do **NOT** need to have a lot of money.*

*You do **NOT** have to be an inventor.*

*You do **NOT** have to take big risks.*

Howard Schultz, who built Starbucks, came from poverty. Bill Gates, who built Microsoft, dropped out of college. Sam Walton did not invent a new business. Ross Perot did not take big risks when he built EDS.

Academic research has shown that there is no correlation between personality, intelligence, book learning, or family pedigree and entrepreneurial success. Moreover, research has taught us that successful entrepreneurs do not have to take big risks and "bet the ranch"; but rather, they test ideas quickly while risking small amounts. Entrepreneurs test their ideas and test the key assumptions that are necessary for business success. They get in the field with potential customers and learn from doing.

So anyone who has the right skills and right temperament and who can sell his or her skills can be an entrepreneur. Age, gender, nationality, country of origin, race, religion, and schooling are not predictive of success or failure.

Successful entrepreneurs are action-oriented—they try their ideas with customers and learn how to improve their products or services. Entrepreneurs are tinkerers. They keep working at it until they get it right for customers.

Customers determine success. To be successful, you need to produce a good product that delivers value to the customer for a fair price. Value means meeting customer needs.

We also know that to be successful you do not need a unique product or service, nor do you need to be smarter than your competition. What you have to do better is (1) listen to your customer and help your customer meet their needs, (2) give your customer great service, and (3) deliver a good product—all for a fair price, fair to the customer and to you.

What have we learned from successful entrepreneurs?

Many successful entrepreneurs came from humble backgrounds and were raised by ambitious parents. Many worked for years in a business before leaving to start their own businesses. And most were not inventors. Most successful entrepreneurs are able to find good opportunities. They find needs that many customers have and then have the courage to take the leap to try to meet those needs on their own.

Good entrepreneurs understand that the customer is always right—so they listen to customers and try to improve their products. They are not stubborn, defensive, or rigid.

> **Business Rule #3:**
> Customers know best what they need.

Good entrepreneurs are also generally good with people. People like doing business with nice people, and employees like working for nice people.

Key Definitions

First, let's agree on some key definitions used throughout the book.

- An *entrepreneur* is anyone who actually starts a new business. Note we said start—not think about, not consider—but actually do it. Entrepreneurs are doers.

  "To do is to be."—Socrates
  "To be is to do."—Plato

- *Entrepreneurship* is the process of building a business. This process is an "act–learn–do it better" process. Entrepreneurs learn as they go. This learning is iterative and incremental.
- A *customer* is anyone with unmet needs who has enough money to pay someone else to meet those needs.
- *Price* is the amount of money you get paid to do something for a customer—or the amount of money a customer is willing to pay you to meet their need.
- *Cost* is the amount of money it costs you to meet the customer's need. Costs include materials, overhead, labor, delivery, billing, installation, heat, lights, rent, taxes, and so on.
- *Profit* equals cash received from a customer less your costs to produce the product or service.
- *Your profit* is what you live on—what you have to spend for rent, mortgage, car, food, lights, clothes, kids, and so on.

Two Common Paths to Entrepreneurial Success

Basically, there are two ways to increase your chances of entrepreneurial success:

1. **Learn the business:** Work in and learn a business before starting a similar business. Learn about the suppliers, the customers, how to operate the business for some years and then go out and start a similar business. Examples: Wal-Mart, Home Depot, Chilis, Starbucks, EDS, Outback Steakhouse, and Intel.

2. ***Start your part-time business:*** Keep your day job and begin your business at nights and on the weekends and build it up before quitting your day job. Example: Ford Motor Company.

Do people "risk it all" and start businesses with little business experience and no customers? Yes. But these occurrences are rarer than you think. Many people lower the risk of starting a business because they begin a business with a customer or customers.

Let's stop here. You should ask yourself these questions:
- What business do I know?
- What am I good at doing?
- What am I not good at doing?
- Do I know any potential customers?
- What do they really need/want?
- Can I give them what they need/want?

Remember the business rules:

Business Rule #1:
The Jerry McGuire Rule: Follow the Money—Cash is King.

Business Rule #2:
The Peter Drucker Rule: "The sole purpose of business is to serve customers."

Business Rule #3:
Customers know best what they need.

Chapter One: Lessons Learned

1. Businesses succeed only by meeting customer needs.
2. Businesses succeed because they make profits.
3. Business profit equals cash in from customer minus cash out for costs.
4. Successful entrepreneurs meet customers' needs better, faster, or cheaper than someone else.
5. IQ, education, family background, race, religion, and ethnic origin are not predictive of entrepreneurial success.

6. Successful serial entrepreneurs are not big risk takers—they take small-measured risks.

7. Most successful entrepreneurs are not inventors or discoverers or geniuses.

8. Business is about people. You need people to buy your product, people to work hard for you, and people to finance your business.

9. Many successful entrepreneurs had previous work experience in the same types of business they started.

10. Many successful entrepreneurs developed their businesses part-time before quitting their paying jobs.

11. Entrepreneurs are *doers*.

12. Entrepreneurs test an idea—they do trials.

13. Entrepreneurs learn and iterate, tinker and get better.

14. Entrepreneurs listen to customers.

15. Entrepreneurs constantly get better and improve their products or services.

chapter two

Basic Rules of Business Success

CHAPTER TOPICS

- *The 8 common start-up mistakes*
  1. *Choosing a bad business opportunity*
  2. *Choosing the wrong customers*
  3. *Choosing the wrong products or services*
  4. *Pricing products or services improperly*
  5. *Not selling to enough customers fast enough*
  6. *Not executing well*
  7. *People problems*
  8. *Mismanaging growth*
- *Basic rules of business success*
- *The 7 Ws*

The 8 Common Start-Up Mistakes

In the following sections, we discuss the 8 common mistakes start-up companies make and use them as a teaching tool to set forth the basic rules of business that successful entrepreneurs use.

Common Mistake #1: Choosing a Bad Business Opportunity

There is a BIG difference between a good *business idea* and a good *business opportunity*.

Ideas are as plentiful as sand on a beach. The entrepreneurial trash cans are full of good ideas—ones for products that work and that make sense. The problem is that customers did not need them badly enough to pay for them.

The difference between a business idea and a business opportunity is two-fold:

1. Good business opportunities satisfy existing customer needs.
2. Customers are willing to now pay for satisfying those needs.

Customers might consider an idea "nice-to-have" but do not see it as necessary.

The second big difference between a good idea and a good business opportunity is that a good idea may not "pencil"—that is, the economics might not work. By that we mean it is unlikely that enough product will sell at a profit large enough for you to earn a living. A good business opportunity pencils—you should be able to make a good profit.

Another reason your good idea may be a bad business opportunity is execution. It may be something hard for you to do or to produce for any number of reasons, or it may be outside your skill level. Or the product may be too complex to be made in bulk with consistent high quality by employees.

Your business idea may not be a good opportunity because you cannot find customers or because there is good competition that you cannot beat either because of cost or quality level issues. Good business opportunities are ones that meet customer "must-haves." There is a specific customer need or "pain" that is met or reduced because of your product or service.

We meet many hopeful entrepreneurs who tell us they have created a new product or they have developed something that is completely new.

Unlikely.

Trust us, in the year 2008, there are very, very few things that you can think of that someone somewhere has not already thought of and tried. That is okay. Uniqueness is not necessary.

> **Business Rule #4:**
> You are looking for a good business opportunity—*not* a good idea.

So what is a good business opportunity? A good business opportunity

1. Has many potential customers with real needs (a large market).
2. Has customers who you can find (customer access).
3. Has customers who have money to buy your product (qualified prospects).
4. Allows you to make and sell your product at a profit (good profit margin).
5. Can result in enough sales to enough customers fast enough (conversion rate).
6. Allows you to earn your needed income level.
7. Is something you are qualified to do.
8. Requires that you do something that someone else is not doing well enough (beatable competition).

Another way to describe a good business opportunity is

- A large potential market, with…
- …Customer access with…
- …Many qualified prospects, with…
- …The potential for a good profit margin, with…
- …The potential for fast enough customer adoption; so…
- …You can earn enough money by…
- …Doing something that you are qualified to do by…
- …Beating the competition.

In Chapter 3, "What Is a Good Business Opportunity?" we will use an approach that is adapted from the brilliant work Discovery Driven Planning did in 1995 by Professors Ian MacMillan of Wharton Business School and Rita McGrath of Columbia University Business School. We can use it to evaluate business ideas and test whether a given idea is a good business opportunity.

Success in the business world is measured by positive cash flow. Positive cash flow results from customers paying you enough for your product that you can cover all your costs plus make a large enough profit that you can make a living.

Common Mistake #2: Choosing the Wrong Customers

To be successful in starting a business, you have to have a match; that is, you have to align the right customers with the right products or services, which then results in the customers' needs being met—which is a large part of the foundation of a successful business. Mistakes can occur by trying to force a "fit" between who you might see as a customer and your product as you produce it. Customers know what they need, and not all potential customers will be real customers. You have to find those customers. *Customer segmentation*, which is discussed in subsequent chapters, is a good tool to use in choosing which customers to go after. *Qualified prospects* will be your goal—those high-priority prospects who have the specific needs you can fulfill and the money to pay you for meeting their needs.

Mismatches occur when you try to sell a potential customer something he or she truly does not need resulting in you having chosen the wrong customer.

Common Mistake #3: The Wrong Product

What is the right product? The right product is that product which gives the customer what he or she needs, no more, at a price they can afford and which allows you to make a fair profit.

Delivery channels will be the means through which you reach and get the most attention from the largest number of qualified potential customers. It could be a retail store, the newspaper, the Internet, a wholesaler, or radio advertising. You will also learn on what basis to make your sales pitch: your *Product Differentiation Story*. How will your product or service be better? Will you compete on price, features, reliability, service, or quality?

Creating a sales pitch as to how your product is different and better requires you to understand your competitors' products. This book shows you how to use a competitor product analysis template, looking at the features, performance, cost, reliability, desirability, style, quality, ease of service, ease of repair, and ease of use of your competitors' product(s).

You will also learn how to choose your "battlefield"—the basis on which you can beat your competition. This entails deciding what your differentiators will be.

Selling the right product is giving the customer enough of what he or she needs but not too much, cost-wise. Customers are willing to pay for what they need—not for what they do not need.

Many entrepreneurs fail the product test because

- They love their product more than they love the customer.
- They want to make the world's best product with all the bells and whistles.
- The customer either does not need or is not willing to pay for all the bells or whistles.

Common Mistake #4: Pricing Products or Services Improperly

- How much will someone pay for your product?
- What price do you need to charge to make a profit?
- How do you determine your costs before you start the business?
- How do customers view pricing?
- What are the two best ways to set your price as a start-up?

Pricing is simple: If you get it wrong, two things can happen, and they both are bad. First, no one will buy your product, or second, you make sales but lose money because your costs exceed your price.

There are three key parts involved in determining your price:

1. Figuring out your product cost—fully loaded. Remember:

Price – Cost = Positive Cash Flow

2. Knowing what your competitor's price is and knowing your potential customers' buying choices.
3. Value-pricing, which is truly understanding what your potential customer is willing to pay for.

In reading about Common Mistake #4, you will learn when your price has to be lower than the competition's, when it is okay to be on par or the same as your competitor, and when you can charge a higher price than your competition.

Common Mistake #5: Not Selling to Enough Customers Fast Enough

Chapter 7, "How Can You Overcome Customer Inertia?" deals with the customer buying process, overcoming customer inertia, and the velocity (speed) of purchase and volume (number) of purchases you need to make to be successful.

We are going to make a bold statement, a true one, but for you probably a shocking one:

> **Business Rule #5:**
> Every entrepreneur over-estimates the number of customers that will buy and the speed at which they will buy.

Why? Because entrepreneurs love their products, and they think everyone will love them as much as they do.

Wrong.

Customer inertia is strong, and people do not like to change their behavior, including their buying habits. Why should your customer change? Why should he or she do something new like buy from you? Chapter 7 discusses how you overcome customer inertia and how you create a sense of urgency to buy.

The second issue we discuss in both Chapters 2 and 7 is the concept of Customer Conversion Rates. You need to accept the fact that all customer prospects will *not* buy your product. How many prospects must you have to convince just *one* of them to buy?

Number of Buyers ÷ Number of Prospects = Customer Conversion Rate

The next variable is how long of a time is the buyer decision process? How long will it take for your prospective buyer to make his decision?

10 minutes?

1 day?

1 week?

1 month?

3 months?

6 months?

1 year?

Wow—big differences.

You will learn that the time to make a sale depends on the magnitude of the price and whether your product has a short lifespan or will last for years. Selling someone a bagel that will last a day is very different from selling someone a car, which will last years. This also impacts the number of customers you will need to be successful—and it impacts the length of time it will take to make a sale.

All of this will teach you a big difference between a high-volume business and low-volume business, which impacts the number of sales you need to make. And you will also learn the difference between low-profit products and high-profit products.

Simply put, you have to sell a lot of low-price, low-margin products to succeed.

Remember: *You will overestimate you number of buyers, AND you will underestimate the length of the buying time.* This combination means that you will not earn as much money as fast as you think.

Common Mistake #6: Not Executing Well

Great—you have customers. Now you have to deliver a quality product on time, every time, defect-free at a profit.

You have to *execute* and *operate* a business, and you probably have never done so.

Chapter 8, "How to Manage Your Business," teaches you some basic management principles—how to understand your *value chain*; how to create *processes*; how to *prioritize* daily tasks and *manage by objectives*; and how to *manage by exceptions* or variances. You will also learn about the *power of simplicity*, the rule of 3s, and the rule of 7s.

Do not be overwhelmed. Most businesses are not rocket science. Running a business is a lot like baking a cake—you need the right ingredients. You need to do steps in the right order. You have to use measured amounts—and you do it the same way every time.

Running a business is "sweating the details" and loving the everyday challenge. But businesses are also composed of people, and people make mistakes. It's is the job of a manager to make good stuff, limit the bad stuff, and fix the mistakes.

Common Mistake #7: People Problems

Business is about *people*. You do business with people: customers, and you do your business in most cases through people: your employees. Your success depends on how your employees treat customers and how your employees do their jobs.

Without good employees doing good work, you will fail—pure and simple.

In Chapter 9, "How Do You Find and Keep Good Employees?" we focus on how to hire, train, and retain good employees and the best practices on how to manage people based on the work done by researchers at the University of Michigan, Harvard, Stanford, Case Western, and at Gallup.

> **Business Rule #6:**
> Happy employees create happy customers, which creates profits for you!

And who creates happy employees? You! As the owner, manager, or boss, *you* create happy employees by the way you treat them.

Do you treat your employees fairly, with respect, give them a sense of doing something important and meaningful, praise them, teach them, help them accomplish their dreams while they help you accomplish yours?

We discuss two fundamental management rules in the People Problems topic:

1. Employees will do what you measure.
2. They will do it even better if you reward what you measure.

Our goal in Chapters 8 and 9 is to teach you how to create a *high performance business*—how to create an environment that promotes high performance. This will help direct your focus on the "why" of your business—so employees can find meaning and pride in being on your team.

And last, we introduce the concept of creating a "family" at work. The second part of the chapter will focus on you—your people skills and how you need to manage not only your employees but also yourself.

Common Mistake #8: Mismanaging Growth

Congratulations—you have customers. Congratulations—you have more customers than you expected.

Success creates challenges. How do you manage your growth so that you do not implode? Success is good. But too much success too fast can overcome the best new business. By overcoming, we mean that big mistakes happen. Common big mistakes are

- Poor quality products
- Missing customer delivery times
- Poor financial controls
- Employee theft
- Employee defection to a competitor
- Employee illegality or misrepresentations
- Hiring too many new employees too fast
- Improper training of employees due to time pressure
- Promoting people before they are ready for the next job

How do you simultaneously, on a daily basis, service existing customers; produce more products and services on a high quality basis for new customers; hire, train, and motivate new employees; all the while managing cash flow? How do you expand when there is a limit to what you can personally do? Do you need to put into place processes, quality controls, financial controls, and technology? How and in what order? Do you need to make investments in computers, people, and software? And yes, we discuss the unthinkable: Are you the right person to manage the business as it grows?

Basic Rules of Business Success

Let us review some of the key business rules that are the foundation of building a successful business.

Business Rule #1:
The Jerry McGuire Rule: Follow the Money—Cash is King.

Business Rule #2:
The Peter Drucker Rule: "The sole purpose of business is to serve customers."

Business Rule #3:
Customers know best what they need.

Business Rule #4:
You are looking for a good business opportunity—*not* a good idea.

Business Rule #5:
Every entrepreneur overestimates the number of customers that will buy and the speed at which they will buy.

Business Rule #6:
Happy employees create happy customers, which creates profits for you!

Business Rule #7: The 7 Ws

A good business opportunity should answer the 7 Ws.

1. **W**hat can I sell?
2. To **W**hom can I sell?
3. **W**hy will customers buy from me?
4. At **W**hat price?
5. **W**hat are my costs?
6. **W**hen will customers buy?
7. **W**hat will the competition do?

Chapter Two: Lessons Learned

Businesses generally fail for 8 fundamental reasons:

1. People choose a bad business opportunity.
2. People try to sell to the wrong customers.
3. People try to sell the wrong products or services.
4. People price their products improperly.
5. People overestimate the number and the speed at which people will buy.
6. People cannot manage the business so as to consistently produce high quality products on time at a profit.
7. Employee problems.
8. People cannot scale their businesses to accommodate customer demand.

Let's move on to Chapter 3, and learn some techniques to evaluate business ideas.

What Is a Good Business Opportunity?

CHAPTER TOPICS

This chapter uses two examples, a sandwich shop and a children's clothing store, to explore the majority of the following topics:

- *Net profit margin and customer conversion rates*
- *Does your business idea "pencil" (make economic sense)?*
- *Determining pricing*
- *Analyzing and learning from your competition*
- *High margin business versus low margin business*
- *Estimating your costs and nailing down the details*
- *Burn rate and breaking even*

This is a chapter you will be able to use over and over until you find the *right* business for *you*. We are going to explore a way of thinking—a template to be used in evaluating business ideas. This method of thinking requires you to understand and keep in mind two key business concepts:

1. **Net Profit Margin**

   Net profit margin is the profit from the sale of a product divided by the sales price of the product. That percentage is a short-hand measure of profitability. Your profit from the *sale of a product* is your sales price minus all the costs to make, sell, and deliver the product.

   If your net profit margin is 20% and you sell a product for $10, then at the end of the day you should make $2.00 profit per sale. However, if your net profit margin is only 5%, then you would only make $.50 profit per sale. This being said, you would have to sell a lot more products with a 5% net profit margin than with a 20% profit margin to earn a $1000 per week profit.

   How many products would you have to sell for $10 with a 20% net profit margin to earn $1000 per week? The answer is 500. But what would be the answer if your net profit margin were 5% instead of 20%?

   That answer is 2,000 products—a *big* difference.

2. **Customer Conversion Ratio**

   Customer conversion ratio is the percentage of customer prospects who actually buy your product. The goal is to make sales pitches to enough prospects so that you make the required number of sales. Prospects become customers when they buy.

   Taking our example in the first point, with a product price of $10 and a net profit margin of %5, you needed to make 2000 sales per week to generate $1000 weekly profit. Well, if your customer conversion ratio is 10%, that means you would have to make 20,000 sales pitches a week—*wow*.

   So conversion ratios help you determine the number of sales pitches you need to make and thus the number of sales people you will need—and the number of customer prospects you need weekly and daily.

The higher the conversion ratio, the lower the number of sales pitches you will need to make. As you will learn later, the best way to increase your customer conversion ratio is to focus on high probability prospects—that is, learn how to determine a prospect's likelihood of becoming a real buyer.

Number of Buying Customers ÷ Number of Attempted Sales = Customer Conversion Ratio

Pencil It

We want to stress the importance of "penciling" your business. Do some preliminary research, and put it all down on paper to the best of your knowledge. Use the tools provided in this chapter. Understanding net profit margin, customer conversion rates, costs, and customer traffic will help you do a back-of-the-envelope mathematical analysis. Think about the following:

- Do you have the expertise or knowledge to produce the product?
- How will you make the product?
- What equipment will you need?
- How can you get customers quickly?
- How will prospects know you are in business?
- Who is your competition, and how will they respond?
- Why will your product sell, and what is your value proposition?
- Will your product be cheaper?
- Will your product be better?
- Will your product be different?
- And so on…

If your business idea pencils, it is worth seriously exploring. You can then do more research and homework, and you're on your way. If your business idea does *not* pencil, find another idea.

Ok, let's explore an example: Let's assume you want to open a sandwich shop that sells sandwiches for lunch, and let's call your new business "The Best Sandwich Shop." What questions do you need to answer to figure out whether this business idea is a good business opportunity?

1. How much money do you need to earn weekly for you and your family?
2. What will be the average sales price for your sandwiches?
3. What will be your fully loaded costs to operate your business?
4. What will be your per sandwich net profit margin?
5. How much profit will that produce per sandwich?
6. How many sandwiches do you need to sell everyday to make a living?
7. How often will customers come into your shop and buy?
8. How many total different customers will you need each week to make your livelihood?

For purposes of this example, we are assuming that

- You know how to make a good sandwich.
- You can get good sandwich meats, produce, and breads.
- You can find a good and affordable location for your shop.
- You can get the necessary state and local food establishment licenses to operate.

Example 1:
The Best Sandwich Shop

The first question you have to ask is: "How much money do you need to earn before income taxes on an annual basis?"

$10,000?

$20,000?

$30,000?

$40,000?

$50,000?

$100,000?

What is your goal? What is the minimum you need? What would be *nice* to earn?

Let's assume (only as an example) that your answer is $40,000 per year before taxes or $800 per week *net profit*, assuming two weeks of vacation and holidays. Ok, how do you make $800 net profit per week?

You sell sandwiches.

How many sandwiches do you need to sell each week? The answer to that question depends on the answers to the following questions:

1. What will be the average sales price for your sandwiches?
2. What will it cost you to make a sandwich, including all your costs for rent, heat, lights, water, insurance, labor, and so on. (This is your total cost to open and run your business weekly divided by the number of sandwich sales per week.)
3. What is your average profit per sandwich: your average sales price minus your average costs per sandwich?
4. Divide $800 by that average profit number. For example, if your average net profit per sandwich is $1.00, you need to sell 800 sandwiches per week or 160 per day.

Now comes the researching and digging for information part. How do you find out what your average sales price per sandwich should be? How do you estimate your operating costs?

What Is the Average Price You Can Sell Your Sandwiches For?

First, think about the kind of sandwiches you want to sell. How many different kinds can there be? Where do people buy those sandwiches now? At what prices do those places sell their sandwiches?

Do your research. Do a survey; visit the competition. Visit sandwich places that have been in business longer than a year. Why? Because if they have lasted for a year or more, they are likely to be profitable. And that means their prices for sandwiches exceed their costs. Good information for you. See if they will give you a copy of their menu or at least their take-out menu. What prices are they asking? Do this for several good sandwich places.

Okay, this is a good start. You have learned two key pieces of information: The competition seems to be making a profit at a certain price point, and it is unlikely you can charge more than they are charging unless you are doing something very different from them.

Let's assume that after all this thinking and research, you determine that you can sell good sandwiches at an average price of $5 per sandwich. So if you need to earn $800 each week, and your sandwiches sell on average for $5 each, how many sandwiches do you need to sell each week?

160?

No!

What common mistake did you make? You forgot the difference between sales price and profit. If you guessed 160 sandwiches, that only meant you would have received $800 dollars from customers. Out of that $800, you have to pay all your operating costs. How much of the $5 sales price will be profit? What will it cost you to make a sandwich ("all-in costs")? All-in costs means your cost of food, employee costs, rent, heat, lights, wrapping paper, paper plates, salt, pepper, cleaning supplies, bathroom supplies, employee taxes, insurance, licenses, and so on.

So, what amount do you *really* need? What will be your profit margin?

Competitors

Competitors are a fact of life. You will have them.

This research should start you thinking about how you can attract customers. For example, if you visit your potential competition, why will their customers change and buy from you? Better quality? Better price? Better location? Will you give customers free potato chips or a free drink? Will your shop be more fun to visit?

Learn from competitors. Visit many, many sandwich shops. Write down what you like about each. Sam Walton built Wal-Mart by visiting competitors and copying good ideas. Take the best ideas from your competitors and make a "better sandwich shop."

But do not forget that your competition will respond. You are attacking their livelihood in building your own, and they will protect their turf either by lowering their prices or improving their product or both. This introduces the concept of sustainable advantage. What, if anything, can you do that will help you keep your customers long-term?

Wow, there are so many things to think about. At this point, there are a couple of short-cuts to finding the answers you need. The first way is public information—looking at sandwich companies that have sold stock to the public such as McDonald's, Burger King, and so on.

Comparables

In most cases, there are big companies (like McDonald's, Burger King, Subway, Quinzos, and Chick-Fil-A) who are already in the sandwich business. Some of them are *public* companies. Public companies must disclose their profit margins.

Using the Internet you can look up those companies and find their websites. Go to McDonald's website and look under Company Information. Then click Investor Relations or Investor Information. Then click on Financials or SEC filings. Under SEC filings, you will link to annual reports, which will contain the company financial statements.

Companies disclose their operating margins—gross and net. You will want to look at *net profit margins*. Look at two or three companies and use the average net profit margin. Understand this is just a guideline and that your profit margin will be different. It may be higher because you will be a smaller business (especially in the sandwich shop business), and you should have fewer costs.

Internet Research

Another research tool is to go on the Internet and search sandwich shops and sandwich shop profits. Almost every type of business has a trade association or cooperative that provides a newsletter. These are a great source of information. Today with the Internet, information is out there if you just look hard enough in enough different places. Be a good detective.

Speak with Other Entrepreneurs

Another way to do research is to go visit some sandwich shops in locations that will not be competitors of yours and speak with the owners. Tell them about your dream and ask for their help. Someone will say, "How can I help you?" Then, you should learn about their operating costs and ask them to share with you the big mistakes they made in starting their businesses. In addition, ask their advice about suppliers, how they advertised, how they were successful.

Entrepreneurs generally want to help other entrepreneurs—especially if they are not future competitors.

Back to the Math

Let's assume for our example that the net profit per sandwich is 18% (or 90¢) a sandwich. That is, you can estimate making 90¢ profit on every sandwich you sell. *How many sandwiches must you sell each day to make $800 per week?*

Profit per week = $800

Profit per sandwich = $.90

Number of sandwiches needed to sell each week = 800/$.90 = 888

Number of sandwiches needed
to sell every day on average = **178** (888/5 days per week = 178)

Is this realistic?

Is this likely?

Let's factor in some more considerations:

1. Yes, there are eight hours in a workday, but lunchtime is not eight hours long. You have a finite timeframe in which to sell 178 sandwiches.

2. Workers only have one hour max to drive, park, come in, order, eat, and go back to work. The location of your shop is critical. Parking is critical. How you design your shop to move people through quickly is critical.

This raises even more questions for you:

- What time will your lunch business begin?
- What time will your lunch business end?
- How many sandwiches can you make per hour? Or will you pre-make them?
- How many times a week will your customers buy from you?
- How many *different* customers will you need a week?

- How far will customers drive for a good sandwich?
- Do enough people work within a reasonable drive time?

Now think how different your answers would be if the business is a low margin business—say, 5% (see Table 3.1).

Table 3.1 *Number of Sandwiches Per Day*

Net Profit Margin	# Sandwiches Per Day
5%	640
10%	320
15%	213
20%	160

At a 20% profit margin, you have to sell 160 sandwiches a day. At a 5% profit margin you have to sell 640 a day—*A BIG DIFFERENCE*.

Now, if a customer comes in twice a week, every week, you will need at least the ratio shown in Table 3.2.

Table 3.2 *Number of Different Customers Per Week*

Net Profit Margin	# Different Customers Per Week
5%	1600
10%	800
15%	533
20%	400

You should now understand why net profit margins are so important. They determine your volume—*the number of customers you need* to be successful. Your conclusion: You will need 533 different customers if the average customer comes in twice a week.

Remember, you will not attract or get all the lunch business in your area. So how many potential lunch customers need to exist? 2000? 4000? 5000? Again, this raises the issue of location. Opening a shop near your apartment in a residential neighborhood is very different than opening a shop in a high employment location. Remember Willy Sutton—when asked why he robbed banks he said,

"Because that is where the money is." Where are your customers? Go where your potential customers are.

The problem with that easy answer is what? You guessed it. Landlords know this. Your rent will be higher in a location near large numbers of workers. So your costs will be higher. This is the *trade-off*. Will the increased rent, though, be offset by more sales, and will the increased rent make it more likely you will succeed? Will the increased rent lower your profit margin from 15% to 12%, or will it lower it from 15% to 5%? That allows you to figure out the impact on the number of sales.

Now let's review. We have gone through a process of figuring out average sales price; figuring out our estimated net profit margin; and figuring out the estimated number of sales we need to make a day, and we have looked at how many repeat customers we may have, which helps us understand the number of potential or prospective customers we may need.

This is the *pencil process*, a method of analysis that gives us a snapshot picture of how much volume we need to do. And we have learned that net profit margin has big consequences in that it dictates the number of customers we need each day.

Let's look at another example—a children's clothing store.

Example 2:
Children's Clothing Shop

Now instead of a sandwich shop, assume you want to open a shop that sells children's clothes. (Ed's parents' first entrepreneurial venture was a children's clothing store.) Assume the average sale is $10.00 per customer with a 15% net profit margin. And let's assume you still want to take home $800 a week before taxes. So how many sales per week do you have to make?

Table 3.3 *Sales Needed Per Day*

$10 x 15%	= 1.50	Net profit per sale
$800/$1.50	= 534	Sales per week
Average sales per day/6 days	89	

Let's now learn about customer conversion ratio.

Customer Conversion Ratio

So you need to make 89 sales per day. Will everyone who comes into your store buy? Of course not. Lots of people will be looking, learning, planning ahead, shopping prices, exploring, or just wasting time. Some people call these non-buying people "tire kickers." So what percentage of people who come into your store will make a purchase on any given day?

Table 3.4 *Results of Different Customer Conversion Ratios*

What % of Prospects Will Buy?	# Sales Per Day	Per Day # Total People Needed	Per Week # Total People Needed
10%	89	890	5340
20%	89	445	2670
50%	89	178	1068

Wow, what a difference! Customer conversion rates have a dramatic impact on determining the likelihood you can achieve your goal of $800 net profit per week.

Customer conversion rates will help you understand the *customer traffic* you need—the number (volume) of potential prospects you need daily to sell the amount you need.

Customer traffic will depend on your location and how easy it is for you to let people know you are in business. The goal of a business location and advertising is to increase customer traffic. The more customer traffic, the more likely you will make sales, assuming your traffic consists of potential buyers. Let's review.

The lower the profit margin, the larger the number of paying customers you will need.

> **Business Rule #8:**
>
> Low Profit Margin =
> High Volume
>
> High Profit Margin =
> Lower Volume

Customer Conversion Rates

Customer conversion rates will tell you how many total prospects you will need to make a sale.

10% conversion = 10 prospects for 1 sale

20% conversion = 5 prospects for 1 sale

How often your customers need to buy your product will give you an estimate of how big your customer base needs to be. Will your customers buy from you weekly, monthly, or only on special occasions?

So in a low profit margin business, you need a lot of customers buying from you. Low customer conversion rates indicate you need numerous customer prospects to come into your business—customer traffic. If customers will need your product or service infrequently, this requires even more customer traffic.

Business Rule #9:

Profits are your goal—
sooner rather than later.

Business Rule #10:

Cash flow is your business's
lifeblood—it is how you pay
your bills.

Two Different Types of Businesses

1. Low Profit Margin

    Or

    Infrequent Buys ⟶ You need lots of customers.

    Or

    Low Customer Conversion Rate

2. High Profit Margin

   Or

   Frequent Customer Purchases $\longrightarrow$ You need a smaller number of customers.

   Or

   High Customer Conversion Rate

The tools you learned in this chapter allow you to discover the number of potential customers and the number of sales you need every day, which gives you a basis from which to make a judgment as to whether an idea is a good opportunity.

Generally, your net profit margin or allowable profit margin range is limited or determined by the type of business you are in. Most businesses selling similar products will make similar or close to the same margins. What does this mean? Your choice of business— the type of business it is—will greatly influence how much money you can or will make.

Because public companies (companies whose stock is sold publicly) have to disclose their numbers, it is possible to compute average net profit margins by type of business (see Table 3.5).

Table 3.5 *Margins by Sector*

Industry Name	After-tax Operating Margin
Apparel	8.49%
Auto Parts	5.47%
Building Materials	9.45%
Computers/Peripherals	7.66%
E-Commerce	7.95%
Educational Services	10.67%
Electronics	5.05%
Environmental	13.15%
Food Processing	7.64%
Food Wholesalers	3.03%
Furniture/Home Furnishings	7.34%

Table 3.5 *Continued*

Industry Name	After-tax Operating Margin
Grocery	3.38%
Healthcare	12.14%
Heavy Construction	2.91%
Home Appliance	6.98%
Homebuilding	5.01%
Household Products	15.12%
Human Resources	3.33%
Information Services	15.49%
Machinery	9.62%
Medical Services	7.79%
Medical Supplies	8.98%
Metal Fabricating	10.41%
Office Equip/Supplies	7.06%
Packaging & Container	9.46%
Paper/Forest	11.12%
Pharmacy Services	1.64%
Restaurant	12.05%
Retail (Special Lines)	6.10%
Retail Automotive	4.69%
Retail Building	7.66%
Retail Store	4.71%
Shoe	8.70%
Toiletries/Cosmetics	8.76%
Wireless Networking	10.67%

Data Used: Value Line database, of 7364 firms
Date of Analysis: Data used is as of January 2008
Source: http://pages.Stern.nyu.edu/~adamodar/New_Home_Page/datafile/margin.html

So what good are these numbers? They may help you choose a business. For over 7000 big businesses in 2005, the average after-tax operating margin was 11.98%. Assuming a 30% average tax rate, the average pre-tax profit margin was around 17%.

Now, your immediate reaction might be that this is simple—choose a higher margin business...

NO! NO! NO!

You should choose the best margin business in which you would have the highest probability of succeeding at. That means:

A business you can do because of expertise, experience, knowledge, and which you would enjoy doing
and
A business for which you have or can get customers.

You have to be able to produce and deliver high-quality products or services on time, defect-free, and for a profit. And because this business will consume most of your waking hours, you should enjoy doing it.

Estimating Your Costs

> **Business Rule #11:**
> Control your costs—spend wisely on the right stuff.

The next step in thinking in more detail about your business idea is drilling down to estimate your total costs to make, sell, and deliver your product or service.

What happens if you overestimate cash coming in and underestimate your costs?

YOU CAN LOSE MONEY!

And you will have to make up that difference (loss) from your savings, a home equity loan, family loans, or selling property.

THIS IS SERIOUS!

That is why we stress: Please, please, do your homework. There is a wealth of information out there, and there's so much available right at your fingertips on the Internet.

What Does Net Profit Margin Tell You About Costs?

100% – Net profit margin = Your projected costs percentage

It gives you the answer! For example, if you are in a 10% net profit margin business, your projected costs are 90% of your *sales price* (assuming you sell enough stuff). So your total cost estimates should add up to 90% of your average sales price.

Example:

1.   Sales Price = $10 per transaction

     Net Profit Margin = 10%

     Your Profit = $1

     Your Costs = $9

     All of your costs added up should approximate $9 per sale, assuming you sell enough to cover all of your costs.

2.   Sales Price = $15 per transaction

     Net Profit Margin = 20%

     Your Profit = $3

     Your Costs = $12

     All of your costs added up should approximate $12, assuming you sell enough to cover all of your costs.

You need to do research and talk to other business people and accountants and create an estimated weekly cost chart (see Table 3.6).

Table 3.6   *Sample Cost Chart*

Expense	Per Monthly Cost	Expense	Per Monthly Cost
Accounting		Inventory	
Advertising		Legal	
Business Supplies		Licenses	
Cost of Supplies		Lights	
Cost to Deliver		Marketing	
Employee Costs		Phone	
Equipment		Rent	
Furniture		Repairs & Maintenance	
Heat		Taxes	
Insurance		Water	

Why Do You Need to Know Your Costs?

There are two main reasons:

1. You will not usually make sales the first day you are in business because there is a *start-up time*—a time in which you are paying expenses without receiving cash from customers.

2. It will take you time to reach *break-even*—that month when your cash in from customers equals your costs for the month.

Business Rule #12:

Know your burn rate—how soon will you run out of money?

Knowing your costs allows you to plan for your *burn rate*—how fast will you burn through the money you have available from yourself and family and friends to start your business.

To emphasize the importance of choosing a good business opportunity before you start your business, remember these basic business rules:

Business Rule #8:
Low Profit Margin = High Volume
High Profit Margin = Lower Volume

Business Rule #9:
Profits are your goal—sooner rather than later.

Business Rule #10:
Cash flow is your business's lifeblood—it is how you pay your bills.

Business Rule #11:
Control your costs—spend wisely on the right stuff.

Business Rule #12:
Know your burn rate—how soon will you run out of money?

7 Ws

The 7 Ws are a good shortcut way to think about business opportunities. Use them as a tool to evaluate whether a business idea is worth exploring seriously:

- **W**hat can I sell?
- To **W**hom can I sell?
- **W**hy will customers buy from me?
- At **W**hat price?
- **W**hat are my costs?
- **W**hen will customers buy?
- **W**hat will the competition do?

Chapter Three: Lessons Learned

1. Business ideas are like sand at the beach—plentiful, but there are few new or unique business ideas.
2. Not every business *idea* will make a good business *opportunity*.
3. Your idea needs to "pencil"—that is, make economic sense.

4. The key "pencil" drivers are:
   - The amount of money you need to make
   - Net profit margin
   - Customer conversion rate
   - Customer traffic volume
   - Speed of sales
   - Customer buying frequency
   - Burn rate and staying power—how much time (money) can you invest until you make a profit?

5. Remember the 7 Ws:
   - **W**hat can I sell?
   - To **W**hom can I sell?
   - **W**hy will customers buy from me?
   - At **W**hat price?
   - **W**hat are my costs?
   - **W**hen will customers buy?
   - **W**hat will the competition do?

6. Common mistakes business starters make:
   - Overestimating the number of customer sales
   - Overestimating how fast people will buy
   - Underestimating their costs
   - Underestimating the competition

7. Owning a low margin business means:
   - You need a lot of customers.
   - Customers need to buy frequently.
   - You will have to operate very efficiently.
   - Your room for financial mistakes or errors will be small.
   - Volume of customer traffic, customer conversion rates, and knowing the competition is very important.

8. Owning a higher margin business generally means:
   - You need fewer customers.
   - Your customers probably will not be frequent buyers.
   - You will need to consistently generate new customer prospects.
   - Customer conversion rates could be low.
   - You need a constant flow of good customer prospects.

9. Your estimated weekly costs help you predict your *burn rate*: the speed at which you will burn through your money. Burn rate tells you how long you can stay in business until you hit break-even.

10. *Break-even* is the point at which your weekly incoming cash equals your costs going out.

chapter four

How Do You Choose the Right Customers?

CHAPTER TOPICS

- *Who are your right customers?*
- *Why do customers buy?*
- *How do you find high-probability prospects?*
- *Doing a market survey*
- *Who is your competition?*
- *How do you do a competitor analysis?*

This chapter, as well as Chapter 5, "How Do You Design Your Product or Service?" will help you answer the 3 Ws:

- *What will I sell?*
- *Who will buy?*
- *Why will they buy?*

The Right Customers

You already know that customers are the lifeblood of every business. And you have learned that most businesses overestimate the speed of finding customers and the number of people who will buy their products or services.

So who are customers? Customers are high-probability prospects who actually buy your product.

Business Rule #13:

Customers are high-probability prospects who actually buy your product.

Who Is a Prospect?

A prospect is anyone who has a need or a want that is motivating him or her to consider buying a product or service. Customers buy to meet needs or to solve a problem—or they buy to satisfy their wants or desires.

You'll remember from our sandwich shop example in Chapter 3, "What Is a Good Business Opportunity?" a prospect will buy a sandwich because he or she is hungry (need) or because they are thinking about the joy of eating that sandwich (want or desire).

All entrepreneurs have restraints such as limited time, money, and people. Because of these restraints, you have to be careful in how you spend your time and money. You need to spend your time and money finding and selling to high-probability prospects who can become your customers.

Business Rule #14:

Focus on high-probability prospects—*not* just anyone willing to listen.

Who Are High-Probability Prospects?

As we stated, customers buy to solve needs or satisfy desires. Customers' needs come from problems, and the importance of any problem is measured by the amount of "pain" associated with it. The greater the pain, the more likely the customer will buy something to relieve the pain.

High-probability prospects have serious needs or desires.

Needs or desires can be categorized by intensity or degree: top priority, high priority, or medium priority:

- **Top Priority**—Those prospects with needs and desires that are top priority have the following traits:
  - Timing of purchase is critical—the sooner the better.
  - Price is not as important of a factor.

  An example of a top priority would be if you are bleeding so badly that you could die if you do not get immediate attention. In that case, you are not likely to take the time to shop hospitals for the best price or for even the best doctors. You need help now!

- **High Priority**—Prospects who have a high priority for specific solutions to a problem or desire are likely to make their purchase decisions in the near future. In most cases, a decision to purchase a solution has been made; the only thing left is to decide which solution to chose. High-priority prospects are likely buyers.

- **Medium Priority**—Prospects who have medium priority needs and wants tend to be price-sensitive and are slow to make a purchase decision.

The greater the need or desire, the more likely you will be able to convert a prospect into a customer. The lower the need or want, the less likely you can convert the prospect into a customer. Therefore, you want to find and focus on high-probability prospects: those with top priority or high priority needs or desires.

> **Business Rule #15:**
> It is easier to convert top- and high-priority prospects to customers than other prospects.

How Do You Find High-Probability Prospects?

The answer is simple: Ask people what they need and want.

The best way to get the information you need is through research. There are two ways to do research. The first way is called primary research, and the second is secondary research.

Primary research is research where you or the people you hire talk *directly* with potential customers. Primary research is asking people questions to learn about their needs or wants and is a great tool—talk to people and learn what they like, dislike, and so on.

Examples of primary research are

- **Market surveys** are surveys that can be performed in person, on the phone, or by mail. They usually include 15 questions or less and provide more accurate information when a large number of people are questioned. Surveys are good tools for determining who are the best prospects for your product or service and how many of these prospects are in your area.
- **Focus groups** are small groups of people who you get together and who are asked specific questions about their needs, wants, and your product.

Secondary research is defined as getting the information you need from sources that have done their own research and either offer it to you for a fee or for free (for example, census information from the government). Consequently, you're getting the answers *indirectly* from the market. The negatives of getting secondary information from the market are that the questions asked may not be the best questions nor asked of the best people. The benefits of secondary information are its lower cost, and you usually can get the information faster. *Because secondary information is either free or low cost and already exists, you should start here.*

Where can you find good secondary research?

The two best avenues of secondary research are to search the Internet for information and to find a trade association that represents either sellers of the product you want to sell or buyers of that product.

> **Business Rule #16:**
>
> Learn about your industry.
> Search the Internet and find
> a relevant trade association.

What are trade associations? *Trade associations* are organizations made up of members—people like you—who are in the same type of business you want to start or people who sell the same product you want to sell.

There are over 20,000 trade associations in the United States. To see if there is an association for you, usually all you have to do is go to the Internet and do a quick search. The overwhelming majority of these associations have their own websites so you can review what they have to offer. To get the research and business information you may find helpful, you might have to join the association, which in most cases is a minimal cost.

So first do your research on the Internet. Find a relevant trade association and then consider doing your primary research.

Primary Research—Doing a Market Survey

There are two ways to do a survey: Do it yourself or hire a market research firm to do it. Whether you do your own survey or you pay a company to do it for you, you will need to determine the questions you want to ask.

CREATING MARKET SURVEY QUESTIONS

What are the best practices for creating your own market survey? First, you need to focus on the goals of your survey. The most common purposes of market surveys are

1. Identifying high priority market needs and wants
2. Determining your target prospects
3. Designing your product or service
4. Identifying the best communication channels to use for marketing

After you define your goals, you should draft questions you think would be valuable to know about your prospects. Do not forget that you will need to include a couple of demographic questions to help you identify the best prospect base.

For example, if your customers are businesses, you might ask their industry, sales volume, number of employees, and so on, and if they are consumers, you might ask questions related to age, income, marital status, and so on.

When developing your questions, try to word them so the customer can answer them with a yes or no or so that the responder can rank the answers on a scale of 1 to 5.

You can use a scale such as

    1 = very unimportant

    2 = unimportant

    3 = neither important or unimportant

    4 = important

    5 = very important

Prioritize the questions you think are the most valuable or that you consider must-haves. Delete any question that you can find the answer to from another source such as through secondary research sources. Make sure that no two questions are really asking the same thing.

Last, since most people are, at most, willing to spend no more than four minutes answering your questions, we recommend that you do not ask more than 15 questions. After you have developed your survey, test it on a number of people you know to see how long it takes to answer. If it takes more than four minutes, you will need to shorten it.

To help you design your survey questions, we have developed the following example.

Example Survey Questions

Let's assume you're thinking about opening a car repair shop. Because there is a lot of competition in the market for repairing cars including car dealers or specialty repair shops like transmissions or brake shops, you want to make sure that there is enough potential customer interest to warrant opening your shop.

In addition to determining if there is enough demand in the market to open your shop, you want to know what types of repairs car owners are most looking for, where the best location would be for your business, and what the best way would be to market to your prospects.

Here are some examples of the type of questions you might want to consider:

Need/Want Questions

- Which of the following choices most closely represents how often you have to bring your car in for repair:

  Never _____

  Rarely _____

  About once every 6 months _____

  Once every 3 months _____

  Almost once a month or more _____

- When you have a problem with you car, do you usually go to the same place to have it repaired?

  Yes _____

  No _____

- Where would that be? _____

- On a scale of 1-5 (with 1 being very unsatisfied to 5 being very satisfied), please answer the following questions:
  - How satisfied are you with your present car repair places? _____
  - How satisfied are you with their prices? _____
- How interested would you be in finding another place that can do all your repairs at a reasonable price?

  Not interested _____

  Somewhat interested _____

  Very interested _____
- What kind of car problems do you experience most? _____
  _____

Demographic Questions

- How many cars do you own?

  0 _____

  1 _____

  2 _____

  3 or more _____
- What kind of car(s) are they, and how old are they?

  1 _____   Age: _____

  2 _____   Age: _____

  3 _____   Age: _____

  4 _____   Age: _____
- What is your marital status?

  Single _____

  Divorced _____

  Married _____

- Who at your house is responsible for making the decision where to get the car repaired?

  You _____

  Spouse/Significant Other _____

  Whoever has the problem _____

- What is your zip code? _____

- Which of the following categories most closely represents your annual household income?

  Less than $25,000 _____

  $25,000-$50,000 _____

  $50,000-$75,000 _____

  Over $75,000 _____

Product Questions

- Would you be likely to try a new repair place for your car if:
  - They guaranteed the lowest price:

    Yes _____

    No _____

    Don't Know _____
  - They guaranteed their work for one year:

    Yes _____

    No _____

    Don't Know _____
  - If you could win a free trip to Disney World for a week:

    Yes _____

    No _____

    Don't Know _____
  - Someone you trusted recommended it:

    Yes _____

    No _____

    Don't Know _____

- If they gave you a rental car if your car repair will take over 3 hours to fix:

   Yes _____

   No _____

   Don't Know _____

Marketing/Advertising Questions

- On a scale of 1-5 (with 1 = never; 3 = sometimes; and 5 = always), how likely are you to read the following:

   Major Area Newspaper _____

   Community Newspaper _____

   Direct Mail _____

   Unsolicited Email _____

TRACKING SURVEY ANSWERS

Before you start asking people your survey questions, you will need a way to track the answers. We recommend that you use an Internet survey tool. There are many you can choose from online (the following are for example only): www.surveymonkey.com, www.zoomerang.com, or www.zapsurvey.com.

These tools are invaluable whether you are planning on doing your survey online, by phone, or in person. They are relatively inexpensive to use, normally less than $100. When you sign up, just follow the directions they give to enter your questions.

Now that you have determined the questions you're going to ask and you have selected a survey tool to record the answers, the next thing you have to do is to determine the following:

1. The number of surveys you will need to complete

2. How many people you will have to contact to make sure you get the number of survey answers you need

3. Where you are going to find the people or get the names of people to contact

4. The most effective way to implement your survey

Let's review each of these items:

1. **How many surveys do you need to complete?**

   Obviously, the larger the sample you use, the more likely your results will be reliable. That said, we recommend as a rule of thumb, that you take the question from your survey that has the most answer choices (taking the questions from the example we just presented, 5 was the largest number of answer options of any question) and multiply that by 20. Given the questions we presented, you would need to receive at least 100 competed surveys (see equation below):

   ## (5 [largest number of answer alternatives] x 20) = 100

   This should provide you with a large enough sample to generate a reasonable level of accuracy. In no case should you have less than 40 completed surveys.

2. **How many people will you have to contact to get the number of completed surveys you require?**

   On average you can assume that only a small percentage of the people you contact will be willing to answer your questions. The actual number depends on how you contact them. If it's in person, on average you will need to talk to 10 to 20 people for everyone that's willing to answer. If the contact is made by phone, you will need to plan on calling—on average—40 to 60 people for every completed survey. If the contact is made by mail or email, you should plan on 100 to 300 per completed survey.

3. **Where do you find the people or get the names of people to contact?**

   The key is to find the right people to ask. The people you are interested in are people who are likely to be prospects. For example, if you're looking to sell car repair services like the example given, you only want to talk to people who own cars. The best way to find the right people to answer your survey is to buy a list of either phone numbers, mailing addresses, or email addresses (if available) of people or businesses that meet your criteria.

   You can purchase a list relatively inexpensively from list companies online (usually around $0.05 to $0.10 per name). The following three are examples of list companies: www.turbo.marketing.info/index.html, www.w3data.com, and www.engmarketingsolutions.com.

In buying a mailing list, make sure you give the company you are buying your list from as much information as you can about the people or businesses you're trying to contact. Doing so will ensure that you get the best list available.

4. **What's the most effective way to implement your survey?**

Your choice of how to best implement your survey will depend on a number of factors. They include cost, time, size of list, and so on.

The key to keeping the cost low and the timing short is to offer an incentive for people to complete your survey. Examples of incentives include entering their names into a contest where they can win something they would find valuable or paying them to complete the survey (usually five to ten dollars) or donating money to the charity of their choice in place of direct payment.

For planning purposes, you should estimate the average cost per completed consumer survey to run from a low of $10 to over $50 depending on length of survey, target market, and respondent incentive offered. The average cost per business survey can run from a low of $25 to over $100 depending on the job level of person you want to talk, the effectiveness of your telemarketer or marketing piece, among other factors.

If you choose to do a survey, try to avoid the months of July, August, November, and December as the response rates tend to be much lower during those months.

The Competition

What do you have to know about your competitors?

Competitors are those people selling products or services that are the same or similar to your offerings. Competitors want the same thing you want: customers.

You are in a race, a competition, with your competitors to get customers who usually only buy a product or service from one place.

> **Business Rule #17:**
>
> If someone buys from one of your competitors, *you lose*, and the competitor wins.

Secondly, to compete and *beat* your competitors, you have to understand what your competitor is selling so you can offer a better product—one that meets customer needs *better*.

So how can you beat the competition?

- Offer the same product at a lower price
- Offer the customer more benefits for the same price
- Perform faster
- Provide higher quality
- Provide better reliability
- Give better service
- Make it easier for the customer to buy

You also need to specifically identify your competitors. Who is selling the same thing you want to sell? Here it gets tricky. You can define your competition broadly or narrowly. If you want to open a bowling alley, what are you selling? Bowling or entertainment? If you think you are only selling bowling, you will look at only bowling alleys as your competition. This is a narrow definition.

However, if you think you are selling entertainment, you will look more broadly at your customers' choices in your geography including miniature golf, games, arcades, movies, and so on.

> **Business Rule #18:**
>
> When in doubt, always define your competition broadly, not narrowly.

To get the kind of information you need about your potential competitors, we recommend you do the following:

- **Search the Internet**—If your competitor is a public company, you can get detailed financial and marketing information by going to its website and downloading an annual report. In addition, whether it's a public company or not, you can search the website for product and company information, product pricing, marketing strategy, payment terms, and selection.

- **Shop your competitors**—To get a good understanding of the strengths and weaknesses of your competitors, try posing as one of their customers. If it makes sense and fits into your budget, buy their products or services so that you get in-depth information about them and see how they work and what's good or bad about them.

- **Ask your competitors for information**—Believe it or not, the best place to get good information about your competitors is from your competitors themselves. That's right, ask them. Start off by asking their salespeople. Their salespeople are trained to answer questions, and they are likely to provide you with the detailed information you request. At minimum, they usually will send you literature on their products and company. If the competitor has a customer service department, call them. They are usually a good place to find out about any new products or services that are likely to be introduced in the future.

- **Analyze the competition's strengths and weaknesses**—After you have gathered information on your competitors, it's time to *analyze it*. Your primary objectives in analyzing the information are to determine the strengths and weaknesses of their product or service offerings and to identify if and where they are not satisfying customers' needs and wants that you have identified.

> **Business Rule #19:**
> Attack competitors' weaknesses.

The best way to analyze the information is to develop a competitive analysis, which is simple to build. First, make a list of the top and high priority customer needs and wants that you have identified from your primary and secondary market research. On a piece of paper, list those customer needs and wants in a column one below the other on the left side of the chart.

Second, on the top, list your major competitors by name horizontally one after the other (see Table 4.1).

Table 4.1   *Competitive Analysis*

Customer Needs/Wants	Competitors						
	A	B	C	D	E	F	G
List 1st Need/Want							
List 2nd Need/Want							
List 3rd Need/Want							

Third, starting with the first need/want on your list, look at each competitor separately and determine if that competitor presently offers any kind of solution for it. If they do not have a solution that addresses that need/want, put a "0" in the box under that competitor's name.

If a competitor has a product or service that addresses that need/want, you will need to enter in that box a number on a scale from 1 to 5 (1 means the product does a very poor job solving that need/want, and 5 means that the product does an excellent job solving that need/want). After you have done this for each competitor, continue the same process for the second need/want until you have either entered a zero or a numerical answer in each box on the page.

Fourth, once you have completed filling in the all the boxes, it is easy to see which needs/wants are not being addressed effectively. To determine this, add up the numbers in the boxes from left to right for each need/want separately. If you do this correctly, you will have a total number for each need/want in your list.

See Table 4.2 for two of the numerical values of the needs/wants.

Table 4.2 *Competitive Analysis with Data*

Competitors								
Customer Needs/Wants	A	B	C	D	E	F	G	Total
1st Need/Want	4	1	3	5	2	4	5	24
2nd Need/Want	1	3	3	2	4	2	3	18

The needs/wants with the *lowest* number are the needs/wants that are *not* being addressed well by your competitors—in Table 4.2, this would be the "2nd Need/Want."

*If you make sure your product meets the same needs met by your competitors **and** that your product meets the unmet need or want, you have a good chance of out-competing your competition.*

This competitor analysis is not a one-time event. Remember you are in a race with competitors for every customer, and there will only be one winner. If you win enough, your competitors will do something to respond to you so they can win. They may lower their prices; they may add or improve their offerings. So you need to reassess their offerings often enough to stay abreast of what your competitor is selling so you can stay competitive. Competitors *will* respond, and you will have to respond to their response and so on. That is the beauty of business. It is not a static game.

> **Business Rule #20:**
> Competitors will respond. Business is like a baseball game—there is always another inning.

In this chapter, we have tried to help you understand why customers buy and have given you tools to find high-quality prospects and to understand your competition. Remember:

Business Rule #13:

Customers are high-probability prospects who actually buy your product.

Business Rule #14:

Focus on high-probability prospects—*not* just anyone willing to listen.

Business Rule #15:

It is easier to convert top- and high-priority prospects to customers than other prospects.

Business Rule #16:

Learn about your industry. Search the Internet and find a relevant trade association.

Business Rule #17:

If someone buys from one of your competitors, *you lose*, and the competitor wins.

Business Rule #18:

When in doubt, always define your competition broadly, not narrowly.

Business Rule #19:

Attack competitors' weaknesses.

Business Rule #20:

Competitors will respond. Business is like a baseball game—there is always another inning.

Chapter Four: Lessons Learned

1. Your company's likelihood for success is directly tied to identifying your prospects' most important needs and wants and then providing a solution that best meets their objectives.

2. Because not all prospects are equally as likely to buy your product or service, it's important that you determine which specific prospects are most interested in buying your product or service and what's different about them from the rest of the market.

   Prospects who are the most likely to buy your product or service are your target market.

3. The benefits of identifying targeted prospects include marketing and advertising savings, more enhanced product or service design, and increased sales.

4. Doing your homework is critical to your success.

5. Talk to people—learn firsthand people's needs/wants.

6. Constantly survey prospects, customers, and the competition.

7. Know your competitors' strengths and weaknesses so that you can take advantage of their limitations and better serve your targeted customers.

8. Your goal is to spend your time on high-probability prospects.

9. You have limited time and money. Do your research, focus, and be disciplined.

chapter five

How Do You Design Your Product or Service?

Chapter Topics

- *Why should you design your product or service?*
- *Give customers what they need—not what you think they need*
- *What is the difference between product features and product benefits?*
- *What does "value" mean to a customer?*
- *The Value Proposition Ratio*
- *A Value Proposition example*
- *Your reason for being*
- *Your competitive advantage*
- *Low innovation*
- *Product design chart*
- *Prototyping your product—doing a test*

Give Customers Only What They Truly Need

Now that you have identified your most likely buyers and their needs or desires, the next step is to create, structure, or design your product or service offering to meet those needs or desires. You have choices in what to offer for sale.

Remember your goal is to offer customers solutions—to solve customer problems or meet customer needs. That is your *value proposition*—the "why" people will buy from you.

> **Business Rule #21:**
> Customers buy solutions, so you must constantly assess what customers really want or need and make sure you give them that—*not* what you think they need, nor more than they need because they will not want to pay for anything they do not need.

Features or Benefits

Products and services are composed of both features and benefits.

Features are the ingredients of a product. They can usually be added or subtracted from a product or service much like different spices can be added to a meal to vary its taste. Features are generally added to a product or service to *enhance it*—to make it better for the customer. *Features are options—not necessities.* Features are add-ons and can be differentiators.

Benefits, on the other hand, are the reason for the product or service to exist in the first place. Benefits are *necessities*. Benefits are your solution to the customer's problems or desires. And benefits solve a problem, reduce "pain," or satisfy a desire.

So you have to offer benefits; features are optional. What features should you offer, if any? In designing your offering, you have to be concerned about *value*.

What Is Value?

If benefits were the only thing that mattered to people, customers would naturally buy products and services that deliver the greatest amount of benefits over those that offer less. For example, the top-of-the line Mercedes (S Class) has a more attractive list of benefits to the vast majority of consumers than does the Honda Civic. Why then did the Honda Civic outsell Mercedes S Class in 2006 in the United States many times over?

The answer is simple; benefits by themselves are not the only variable in a customer's purchase decision. The other equally as important factor is *price*. The price customers are willing to pay acts as a counterbalance to value. Customers want the best value they can afford.

Business Rule #22:

The goal is to deliver the most value to your customer at a price that is both affordable for your customer and profitable for you.

To help you measure your product or service's value, the following formula was developed. It is called the *Value Proposition Ratio* (see below):

Value = Benefits ÷ Cost

Because value is a function of both benefits and cost, they both have to be taken into account when measuring a product or service's value to customers.

The value proposition gives you an effective way to compare your product or service to those of your competitors. The larger the Value Proposition Ratio is, the greater the value.

Why is it necessary to compare products or services to one another? The reason is simple: You need to do this so you can determine how attractive your product or service is relative to your competitors'. The greater your perceived value, the more attractive your product or service will be and the more likely customers will buy it.

> **Business Rule #23:**
> The key is the value per-
> ceived by the customer.

To be successful, your product or service has to be the most attractive alternative to a large enough number of customers so that you can make a profit. Because this concept can be a little confusing, we have developed the following example to show you how to use the Value Proposition Ratio to increase the attractiveness of a product or service.

Example: Enhancing Your Product/Service Value

For this example, we're going to assume that a new company (we will call it NewCo) is going to build brick homes in the $250,000 price range. NewCo will be building its homes in the same subdivision as two other well-known and highly respected builders in the market, who are also going to sell their brick homes for $250,000.

All three companies are building 2,000 square foot houses with similar floor plans that include 3 bedrooms and 2 bathrooms. NewCo and its two competitors have all allocated an identical $50,000 per house for amenities, and all three builders have a 10% profit margin built into their house pricing.

If NewCo does not do anything differently, it is less likely to sell homes than either of its competitors because NewCo has no reputation in the market, while its competitors are proven and well respected—which customers value. NewCo's challenge raises these questions:

- What could NewCo do to make its product more attractive to buyers than its two competitors?

- How can NewCo design its offering to provide more value without increasing the cost to the customer?
- How can NewCo give customers more of what they want at the same price as the competition and still make a fair profit?

NewCo has three primary options for increasing its product's value to make it more competitive. It can

1. Lower its price.
2. Increase the money it spends on amenities, which will reduce its profit.
3. Offer a more attractive set of amenities than its competitors for the same $50,000 cost.

If NewCo chooses to either lower its price or increase its costs, its profit will decline. If it has to increase its costs or lower its price by more than 10% to be competitive, the company will not be able to make a profit or stay in business. So alternatives (1) and (2) are not viable.

Therefore NewCo's best alternative is to identify a more attractive set of amenities that the company can deliver at the same cost to the customer. That is the essence of product design. Offer more of what the customer truly needs or wants at the same costs and get rid of features or amenities that customers do not perceive as high value-add.

How can NewCo do this?

It has to ask its customers, "What do you really want or need, and what do you value the most?" NewCo (and you) have to do your homework—do your research and get customers to focus on what they truly want and need. NewCo did this by utilizing a combination of focus groups and a market survey. They used the focus groups to help them develop the best questions for their survey, and they used the survey to get an accurate picture of what amenities customers really wanted.

The two most important set of questions in the NewCo survey were

1. How much were customers willing to pay for each of eighteen different amenity options? The amenities they presented included but were not limited to: wood floors, stainless steel appliances, granite countertops, and stone fireplaces.

2. How much were people willing to pay extra for a house if it was built by Competitor A, Competitor B, or NewCo? They asked this question to measure the value of the competitors' reputations and track records versus NewCo being a new company with an unproven track record.

With the results obtained from the survey, it calculated the value people attributed to each of seven different amenity package offerings. Two of these packages represented what their competitors were offering in their houses, and five were new amenity package options NewCo had created using input from their focus groups.

Table 5.1 shows the results of the research. Keep in mind each amenity package actually costs the same—$50,000. The numbers that follow represent the perceived value in the minds of potential buyers.

Table 5.1 *Perceived Value*

Amenity Packages	Perceived Value by Customers	Cost
Package 1 (New Amenity Package 1)	$52,222	$50,000
Package 2 (New Amenity Package 2)	$65,556	$50,000
Package 3 (New Amenity Package 3)	$87,778	$50,000
Package 4 (New Amenity Package 4)	$46,678	$50,000
Package 5 (New Amenity Package 5)	$81,111	$50,000
Package 6 (Competitor A)	$58,889	$50,000
Package 7 (Competitor B)	$62,778	$50,000

Notice the differences in perceived value by the potential customers. Keep in mind all the amenity offerings cost the same $50,000 to build or install. But they have very different perceived values: from a low perceived value of $46,678 to the high of $87,778.

BINGO. You have solved the value proposition.

Because Amenity Package 3 delivers the most perceived value ($87,778), and it costs the same $50,000 to build, NewCo chose it to include in its houses. To determine if this was going to be enough to make its houses the most attractive in its market, it used the Value Proposition Ratio to calculate the relative value of all three builders' homes and then compared them (see Table 5.2).

Table 5.2   *Comparison of Value Proposition Ratios*

Benefits	Competitor A	Competitor B	Competitor C
2,000 Square Feet	$208,500	$208,500	$208,500
Perceived Value of Amenities	$58,889	$62,778	$87,778
Perceived Value of Reputation	$3,850*	$2,050*	$168*
Total Benefits	$271,239	$273,328	$296,446
Customer Cost	$250,000	$250,000	$250,000
Value Proposition Ratio	1.085	1.093	1.186

* Determined using NewCo market survey.

Remember in evaluating the Value Proposition Ratio, the largest number wins. The NewCo home should win because it will deliver more perceived value ($296,446 for the $250,000 purchase price) than the competition delivers.

NewCo in this example was able to offer a better product at the same cost as the competition.

However, there is nothing to stop either of NewCo's competitors from either copying NewCo's amenity package in the future or even doing more detailed research to develop their own more attractive amenity packages. NewCo's lead over its competitors, therefore, is not one they will likely be able to defend long-term and as a result, is likely to be short-lived. To survive and thrive in the future, they will have to find another reason for customers to choose them over their competitors.

To win in the marketplace, you have to constantly improve your service or product offering to stay ahead of the competition.

Business Rule #24:

Avoid the Winner's Curse: Do not think you will continue winning forever. Do not become complacent or overconfident.

How do you stay ahead of the competition and avoid the Winner's Curse?

What is the reason your company should exist in the market in the first place? What is it that you can do better than your competitors? If you cannot find a way to do something better than your competitors do it—bringing something to the table that your customers will value long-term—you will likely fail.

Your "Reason for Being"

Your business must have a purpose for existing in customers' minds. This "reason for being" is your *differentiator*. It is what makes you valuable to the customer and how you differ from your competition.

To help you determine your company's reason for being, we have listed some of the more common reasons for being that companies use to be successful:

- Offering the lowest prices in the market
- Making the product/service the easiest to use
- Providing the best guarantee in the market
- Delivering the best service
- Offering the most attractive financing options
- Providing the largest selection of products/services
- Offering the longest business hours in the market
- Offering to deliver when competitors do not
- Offering the highest quality
- Being the most reliable—doing what you say

So in thinking about your product offering, not only should you focus on the *benefits* you will offer to customers, you also need to think about how you will offer them—with what services or guarantees or with what delivery options that will make you different from the competition.

What will be your reason for being? What will your name or brand mean or stand for? Will you stand for quality, reliability, being the lowest cost alternative, being the fastest, being the easiest to deal with, being the best? WHAT WILL YOUR BUSINESS STAND FOR?

Good businesses design or create a total offering that they execute 99% of the time on time and defect-free. They focus on doing what they are good at, and they execute better than the competition.

> **Business Rule #25:**
> This is the competitive advantage you are seeking: to offer more value at an affordable price and do it defect-free, on time, and with good service every time.

The goal is to create that image of who you are in your customer's mind through your product or service offering and how you do business.

Here are some examples of some well-known companies and their competitive designs:

- **Wal-Mart's** competitive advantage is its lower prices and large selection. It has a competitive advantage because it is the largest buyer of products in the world, and it does everything it can to keep its prices the lowest in the industry. As such, Wal-Mart can sell its products for lower than anyone else and still make a good profit.

- **Pfizer Pharmaceutical Company's** competitive advantage is its exclusive rights to certain medicines and its ability to get physicians to prescribe it. It is able to sell a medicine like Celebrex at a substantial margin because of the patents it has. Legally, this constrains its competitors from competing directly against it. In addition, Pfizer has thousands of pharmaceutical representatives who market Celebrex to physicians every day.

- **Google's** competitive advantages are its top-of-the-mind name recognition and its proprietary Internet search capabilities. In addition, Google's highly attractive and high-priced stock enables it to quickly and easily purchase add-on businesses that leverage its position in the market and its long-term profitability. Given all these strengths it would be extremely difficult for a competitor to beat it.

Now, just because we showed some of the most successful companies in the world, do not assume that only large companies can have competitive advantages. After all, competitive advantages are the reason why small companies get big.

Low Innovation

There is one more very important point that we need to make before you start designing your company's products or services, and that is the following:

A new or small business is much more likely to be successful if it takes a proven product in the market and makes small changes to it that customers say they want. This product design process is called low innovation.

Many great businesses have been built taking things competitors do plus putting them together in a new offering. Learn from your competitors and your customers. You can even design a business by taking good ideas from several competitors. Improvements are easier to do than creating wholly new products for which there is no proven market demand.

In contrast, new or small businesses that offer high innovation products or services that are totally new and unique to their market are much more likely to fail. The key to making the right changes to products/services in the market are

- To first make sure your customer will truly value the changes you are considering
- To be certain that the changes you make are affordable for the customer AND allow you to make a fair profit.

Table 5.3 shows examples of three well-known products and successful product enhancements that have been made to these popular products along with examples of enhancements that could still be made.

Table 5.3 *Product Enhancements*

Product	Enhancements Already Made	Possible New Enhancements
Soft Drinks	Caffeine Free Extra Caffeine No Calories	Vitamin Enhanced Dessert Drinks You Heat It Up
Sofa/Couches	Turns into a Bed Stain Guard Same Day Delivery	Expands to Increase Seating Push-of-a-Button Pattern Changes Built-in Seat Warmers
Televisions	Surround Sound Digital Hangs on Wall	Smell-A-Vision Channels Change Using Voice Command Waterproof—Can Be Watched in the Shower

It's Now Time to Build Your Product/Service

Now that you know the basics for building a product or service, it's time for you to design yours. To help you with this process, we have developed the following Product/Service Design Chart (see Table 5.4).

Table 5.4 *Product/Service Design Chart*

Product or Service Name	Customer Needs/Wants	Reasons for Being	Your Product Benefits	Your Product Features
Your Product or Service				

To increase your likelihood for building a successful product or service, it's necessary to complete the following product design steps in the following order:

1. First, list the highest priority customer needs and/or wants that you have identified from your market research and from your experience in the market in the Customer Needs/Wants column.

2. Second, list all the reasons why your business should exist in the market relative to the needs and wants you just listed and relative to what your competitors are presently offering in the Reason for Being column. What will your business stand for or represent?

3. Next, in the Product Benefits column list all the major benefits your product or service is going to offer that satisfy customers' needs and wants.

4. Finally, list all the features that you will include in your product or service offering in the Product Features column.

Can You Build or Produce It?

Now that you know what the design of your product/service will look like, it's time to turn your attention to how your company is going to build it. To help you do this, we have developed the following set of questions for you to consider prior to building your product/service:

1. Can you build it?
   - What expertise do you need that you do not have?
   - If you need outside assistance, do you know where to get it?
2. How much will it cost, and how long will it take you to build?
3. Is it better to build it yourself or to buy it from someone else who can do it better?
   - If you're going to buy it from someone else, who?
   - How much will they charge?
   - What kind of capacity do they have?

After you have answered these questions to your satisfaction, you are ready to build your company's "first" version of your product or service. Why a "first" version? The next section answers this question.

The Prototype—The Test

The reason for a "first version" is so you can test your product/service in the market with actual customers to make sure you have exactly what they want. If you do not test your product/service before you start spending money on marketing and selling it, you are likely to waste valuable time and money by offering a less attractive product or services than what the market really wants.

The process of testing a new product or service is called a *prototype* or *beta test*.

What Is a Prototype and How Does It Work?

A prototype is a company's first real-world trial of its product(s) or service(s) by a set of customers who have agreed to use the product/service to identify issues and make recommendations.

While it will delay your market introduction somewhat, it is well worth it. Once completed, your final product will be more marketable, and you will be less likely to waste valuable time and money trying to sell a product/service that does not exactly meet the market needs.

The benefits of a prototype include learning and getting feedback from customers, which can lead to:

- Product improvements
- Customer references

Other Tips

While there have been whole books written on product design, we are only able to allocate one chapter to this subject. As such, we have developed the following list of other tips that you should consider when building your product or service:

> **Business Rule #26:**
> Don't fall in love with your product or service. Be willing to listen to negative feedback and change.

- When you fall in love with your product or service, you lose perspective. You find reasons and/or excuses not to listen to your customers' feedback.

Business Rule #27:
Rarely is it the product or service that is the reason for success in a new business. In reality, it is the execution of the business that is the primary driver of a new venture's success.

- Get your product or service out into your market as soon as possible. It is better to come out with a product or service that does not have all of its benefits in place and get market feedback than it is to wait to make your product or service perfect.
  - The longer it takes you to get your product/service to the market, the less likely you will be successful.
  - After you get your product or service into the market, you will start getting valuable feedback.
  - Feedback can be used if needed to modify your product or service to better meet the customers' needs and wants.
  - The longer you take to get your product or service out into the market, the more money you will have spent, and the less you will have available if you should need to change it relative to market response.
  - Rarely do the overwhelming majority of products or services come out perfect when they are first introduced.

Business Rule #28:
Get good customer references as soon as you can. Use them to sell to other customers.

- New and small companies rarely have the dollars to spend on advertising required to build a brand.

- A brand effectively gives a company a seal of approval and, consequently, an advantage over nonbranded or unknown companies in selling their products.

- Quality customer references reduce the risk of buying from an unknown company. Therefore, they are the first step in building a company's brand without having to spend millions in marketing in the process.

This chapter is chock full of good rules to remember about how to design your product or service to create the best differentiating value proposition for your customers. What you want to do is offer more value than your competition or the same value at a lower price. Remember:

Business Rule #21:
Customers buy solutions, so you must constantly assess what customers really want or need and make sure you give them that—*not* what you think they need, nor more than they need because they will not want to pay for anything they do not need.

Business Rule #22:
The goal is to deliver the most value to your customer at a price that is both affordable for your customer and profitable for you.

Business Rule #23:
The key is the value perceived by the customer.

Business Rule #24:
Avoid the Winner's Curse: Do not think you will continue winning forever. Do not become complacent or overconfident.

Business Rule #25:
This is the competitive advantage you are seeking: to offer more value at an affordable price and do it defect-free, on time, and with good service every time.

Business Rule #26:
Don't fall in love with your product or service. Be willing to listen to negative feedback and change.

Business Rule #27:
Rarely is it the product or service that is the reason for success in a new business. In reality, it is the execution of the business that is the primary driver of a new venture's success.

Business Rule #28:
Get good customer references as soon as you can. Use them to sell to other customers.

3 Ws

The 3 Ws are a shorthand strategy. They keep you focused on what really is important and, hopefully, you will stay focused on the essence of business: meeting customer needs. Remember:

- **W**hat will I sell?
- **W**ho will buy?
- **W**hy will they buy?

Chapter Five: Lessons Learned

1. Customers buy solutions, so you must constantly assess what customers really want or need and make sure you give them that—*not* what you think they need nor more than they need because they will not want to pay for anything they do not need.

2. The goal is to deliver the most value to your customer at a cost that is both affordable for your customer and profitable for you.

3. Avoid the Winner's Curse—overconfidence and complacency.

4. The competitive advantage you are seeking is to offer more value at an affordable price and do it defect-free, on time, and with good service every time.

5. Don't fall in love with your product or service—that is the job of your customers.

6. Go to market as fast as possible—learn from your customers.

7. Get customer references as soon as you can—they will help you make more sales.

8. Product benefits are necessities. Product features are options.

9. The Value Proposition Ratio is Value = Benefits ÷ Costs.

10. Value is what the customer perceives it to be—not what you think it is.

11. Your "reason for being" is your essence, your differentiator, and what your business stands for in the minds of customers.

12. Low innovation product design is less risky than a developing a totally new product.

13. Remember you have to be able to build or produce your product reliably and 99% defect-free, on time, and at a profit.

14. Develop a prototype and get in the market quickly and learn from your customers. Test and learn, and adapt and improve. Constant improvement is key.

What Is the Right Price for Your Product or Service?

CHAPTER TOPICS

- *Why is price important?*
- *Profit = Sales Price – Costs*
- *Variable costs and fixed costs*
- *Cost plus pricing or competitive pricing*
- *Break-even: How do you cover your costs?*
- *The use of payment terms, discounts, guarantees, and sales*

The price you pick for your product and/or service is one of the most important factors in building a successful business. The price you pick impacts

- Whether customers will buy your product
- The positioning of your product against your competition
- Your business's profitability

First things first: When setting your product/service's price, there are certain rules you have to understand. The most important one is that you need to have a good idea of what your costs are before you can even begin considering setting your price. If you do not know your estimated costs, you will not be able to determine a price that should produce a profit. Remember:

Profit = Sales Price – Costs

How do you determine your costs? There are two types of costs, variable and fixed. All costs are either variable or fixed in all businesses. *Variable costs* are those costs that vary in amount depending on how much you sell or produce. Variable costs depend on your volume. In the case of our sandwich shop from Chapter 3, "What Is a Good Business Opportunity?" variable costs include food supplies, paper plates, napkins, trash bags, and so on, which will vary with the volume of sandwiches made. *Fixed costs,* on the other hand, are costs that are fixed and do not fluctuate regardless of how much product/service you sell. Examples of fixed costs are rent, management fixed salaries, marketing, salespeople base salaries, phone, and so on.

To estimate your costs, you need to first add up all your fixed costs. These are costs that are not going to change for at least one year no matter how much you sell. The following is a list of the most common fixed costs a new business may have (remember your business might not have all of them, or you could have others specific to your business):

- Monthly rent
- Monthly fixed salaries and employee benefits and taxes
- Monthly phone/cable/DSL costs
- Average monthly business property and casualty insurances
- Monthly lease amounts for furniture, equipment, and/or autos

After you have determined how much your fixed costs are per month, you need to turn your attention to your variable costs. As we just discussed, variable costs fluctuate with your sales volume and tend to change as frequently as monthly. The following is a list of common variable costs in a business. Variable costs tend to differ widely by type of business, and as such these are only examples:

- Product costs
  - Cost of goods you purchased and resold that month or the direct cost of making the product you sold
- Utility costs
- Sales commissions
- Bonuses
- Travel and entertainment costs
- Office supplies
- Miscellaneous expenses that vary monthly

Your monthly costs equal your monthly fixed costs plus your monthly variable costs.

So, now how do you determine your sales price? Basically, for a new start-up, there are two basic ways: cost plus pricing or competition pricing.

Cost plus pricing is one of the two most common pricing strategies used today by new businesses. It is done by first determining what it really costs your company to produce or make your product/service. This is known as your *fully loaded cost*.

To calculate fully loaded cost for your product/service, you add the variable costs you paid for the product/service plus a proportional fixed overhead cost. To determine a proportional fixed overhead cost per product/service, you add up all your fixed costs for the year and divide it by the number of products/services you hope to sell that year. If, for example, your total fixed cost for the year is $180,000 and you're planning on selling 3,000 products, your proportional fixed overhead cost per product would be $60 ($180,000/3,000 = $60).

Then you need to add that $60 to your variable costs, the costs associated with making the product: materials, purchased components, wrapping, shipping, delivery, installation, and so on. After you have determined that fully loaded cost, you add to it a profit margin. If, for example, you want to make $45,000 in profit for the year, you would add $15 for your profit ($45,000/3,000 = $15).

Assuming your variable cost per product is $40, your total product price would be

Variable Cost:	$ 40
Proportional Fixed Cost:	$ 60
Profit Margin:	$ 15
Total Product/Service Price:	$115

You are rightfully asking, "How do I estimate my costs when I do not know how much I am going to sell?" Therefore, how do I set my price?

Well, you make your best guess and as you get experience you learn and reset your price as needed. Or you get your customer to agree to pay a price equal to your actual cost plus a negotiated profit. This is hard to do in a retail environment but easier to do in a service environment. As an example, Ed just had some book-cases built in his house. His carpenter wanted to do it on a cost plus basis. Ed paid for the cost of the materials—lumber, finish, hooks, and so on, and the carpenter charged $35 an hour as his profit.

If you adopt the cost plus pricing method, the first thing the customer will want is an estimate of the final price, and then in some cases he or she will ask you to guarantee that price. That is, if you underestimate your costs, you are responsible for the cost overrun. Both are fair requests, and they put the responsibility upon you to know your costs and your business.

Our experience is that this is very hard to get right in the beginning. Most people make their best estimate and learn as they go from their first sales. Then with better information, they are able to set better prices because they then have real information on costs.

Competitive Pricing

The other most common pricing strategy used by new and small businesses is competitive pricing. Without a doubt, this is the easiest pricing strategy to use. Competitive pricing means you determine your price based on what your competitors charge.

To do this, first you have to identify your most likely competitors. Then you need to find out what they charge for their products/services that are the most like yours. You need to compare your product/service as honestly as possible to theirs. If your product is better—includes more features or better materials or delivers more benefits, you may be able to charge more. But when your product is less competitive, you probably will want to charge less than what that competitor is charging.

The theory behind competition pricing is that if the competitor is still in business, he or she must be making a profit at the prices he or she is charging, and so should you.

Break-even Formula

The break-even formula is an extremely valuable tool. With it you will be able to determine how much you will have to sell to cover all your costs (no profit), given the price you plan on charging. After you have calculated the number of units you need to sell to break even, you need to determine if you reasonably think you can sell at least that amount. If you're not comfortable that you can sell at least that much, you have three choices:

1. You can raise your price. This will lower the total number of units you will need to sell. However, a note of caution: Increasing price may negatively impact the attractiveness of your product/service to your customers and reduce your ability to make sales.

2. You will need to lower your fixed costs. The more fixed costs you can cut out of the business, the fewer units you will need to sell. Be careful here; you should only cut costs that won't negatively impact your business.

3. Find another business opportunity.

To determine how much you need to sell to break even, you need to know
- Your fixed costs per year
- The price you're planning on charging for your product/service
- The variable costs for your product/service

Number of Products Required to Be Sold to Break Even

Assumptions:

- Your company's fixed costs are $200,000 per year.
- The price you are planning to charge is $128.50 per product.
- Your variable cost per product is $23.50.

$$\$128.50 \text{ (price)} - \$23.50 \text{ (variable cost)} =$$
$$\$200,000 \div \$105.00$$

$$= 1{,}905 \text{ units}$$

In this example, your company would need to sell 1,905 units just to break even per year given the price you're charging. That is a gut check for you.

Additional Pricing Factors

One of the most important keys to an effective pricing strategy and business success is making it as easy as possible for your customers to purchase your product or service. To that end, there are a number of other pricing-related factors that you can use to influence customers purchasing besides just price.

The answer to choosing the right factor(s) to use for your business is in understanding what really drives your customers' purchase decisions. The following are just some examples of what drives different customer purchasing decisions:

- Because many customers use financing these days instead of purchasing products/services for cash, there is a segment of customers that are more concerned about how much their monthly payment is going to be than the actual price of the product/service. We call this segment *Monthly Payment Customers*.

- There are other potential customers who do not have the money now in their budget to purchase the product/service. They are more concerned about the timing of when they have to pay than they are with the price. We call this segment *Timing of Payment Customers*.

- There is also a different customer segment in the market who are more concerned about minimizing the risks associated with purchasing a new product/service than they are with price. We call this segment *Risk-Adverse Customers*.

After you have identified what's important to your customers in making their purchase decisions, you're ready to start developing your pricing strategy. The following are some real-world examples of companies that have developed pricing strategies to meet their specific customer requirements. These specific pricing strategies are credited with helping maximize each of the following companies' sales and profitability:

Monthly Payment Amount Driven:
- Below market or no interest rate financing
  - Automobile companies
  - Furniture stores
  - Appliance stores

Pricing Tied to Actual Usage (companies offering price discounts for high-volume users):
- AT&T volume discounts.
- Comcast gives discounts to customers who use more than two of their available services.

Timing or Payment Driven:
- First payments delayed six months or more
  - Rooms To Go
  - New office/apartment leases with long-term contracts

Risk-Adverse Driven:
- Free trial periods
  - Salesforce.com
  - Norton.com
- Fixed fee pricing (get all you use for one set monthly fee):
  - Metro PCS—cellular phone company
  - Vonage
  - Gas Utility Companies—SCANA Energy

- Money-back guarantees
  - Mail order diet products/specialty vitamins
  - Infomercials
  - Software—PeopleSoft

Now before you start thinking about different payment option alternatives, you need to remember Business Rule #1:

> **Business Rule #1:**
> The Jerry McGuire Rule:
> Follow the Money—Cash
> is King.

When considering offering extended payment options, do not forget that you still have fixed and variable costs to pay. **If you do not pay them, you will not be able to stay in business long.** The only way you may be able to take advantage of one or more of these payment options is to identify a company that would be willing to finance your customers' deferred payments, assuming your customers have good credit. There are companies that will pay you upfront and offer financing to your customers, but it will cost you money. Whether this makes sense or not depends on the incremental sales you're able to make. In other words, if you use these techniques to generate sales, your profit will be less. To earn what you need to earn, you will need to sell more. Therefore, these techniques only work if they will help you sell more products.

Chapter Six: Lessons Learned

1. Price impacts your volume of sales and your profit.
2. Profit = Sales Price – Costs
3. There are two types of costs: fixed and variable.
4. Variable costs vary with your volume of product sold.
5. Review your costs monthly.

6. Price also determines your break-even volume—the amount you need to sell to earn enough profit to cover your costs.

7. Cost plus pricing and competitive pricing are two good pricing strategies.

8. You may have to offer guarantees or payment terms to certain customers.

9. Remember—to you, cash is king.

chapter seven

How Can You Overcome Customer Inertia?

CHAPTER TOPICS

- *Customer inertia—the fear of change*
- *Selling is overcoming the obstacles to a sale*
- *Nine common reasons people do not buy*
- *Seven techniques to get a customer to try your product*
- *The key to selling is listening*
- *The psychology of selling*
- *The customer-buying timeline*
- *Selling is like fishing*
- *Reward customer referrals and loyalty*

By now you have learned that when starting a business you need paying customers fast—to cover your costs. You only have so much money to invest in your business, and you have to pay your fixed costs whether you make sales or not.

So you need customers *yesterday*. But you will learn that most customers do not have the same urgency to act as you do.

Most likely, a sale of your product requires people to change because it is unlikely that you will be selling something that no one else sells. Change is hard for most people; change takes time, and people have to get comfortable. People have to work through their hesitance and fear of change. But you do not have a great deal of time—you have expenses every day. So how do you get people to change and buy your product or service *quickly*?

You have to create a sense of urgency.

Yes, people are hesitant to change and are scared that change may be bad for them. This is your challenge to overcome.

> **Business Rule #29:**
> Selling is overcoming obstacles to a sale.

Obstacles to a Sale

Making a sale is a process of overcoming obstacles. People generally will not tell you they are afraid to change—no one admits that to strangers. No, they will give you reasons or excuses why they will not buy. These are the *obstacles* or hurdles that you have to overcome to make a sale. What do you have to do to overcome these obstacles?

- First you have to ask your customers questions about what their problems, needs, or goals are. You have to understand their needs and understand why their current solutions are or are not working. Are they satisfied or not? If not, why? Poor quality? Unreliable delivery? Poor service? Invoice mistakes? Too expensive?

- You have to ask them what it would take for them to change. What does your product have to do?

- Then you have to shape your sales pitch into solving the customers' needs, stressing the benefit of your product—what it will allow your customers to do better, faster, or cheaper.

- Then you have to ask for feedback—ask questions to draw out the obstacles to sale.

- Then you have to drill down with questions to try to understand the *real* obstacles to sale.

- Then you have to overcome them by explaining how buying your product accomplishes customers' objectives, meets their needs, and is not a big risk to try.

The sales process should be an interactive *conversation* with the customer—not a speech by you, and it takes two key skills:

1. Listening
2. Being a good detective

Business Rule #30:
You cannot listen when you are talking.

Business Rule #31:
You will make few sales convincing buyers you are smarter than they are or that you know their businesses better than they do.

The Risks of Buying from You

To address and overcome the obstacles to sale, you need to understand them. The obstacles to sale are often one or more of the following:

- Your product is unproven—how do your customers know it will work?

- You do not have a pool of satisfied customers who can vouch for your product.

- Your business is small—you may not be in business in six months— then how can customers depend on you?

- You have few employees. How can a customer get quick service if he or she has a problem with your product?

- To change to your product means a customer has to change to other products as well—why should they?

- They are not that unhappy with their current vendors.

- You are too expensive.

- Their current vendors are relatives.

- Your product does not improve their situations that much.

You need answers to their concerns, and you have to answer them directly and honestly.

Over time, you will build a "tool box" of ways to sell. You will enjoy the challenge, and you will become comfortable with the fact that you will not be successful every time. You will understand that it takes different approaches with different prospects—that people make sales decisions at different paces—and that some people just are not ready to buy.

The key is to learn as quickly as possible what the obstacles to sale are for you.

When someone gives you reasons why they do not want to buy, be sure to get all the reasons out on the table before you really start selling. Do not let the prospect "faucet" you—do not let the prospect keep dripping obstacles after you solve some by asking them:

- "Are these *all* of your concerns?"

- "Before I address your concerns, are there any others?"

- "Do I understand that the key reasons you have concern are 1, 2, and 3?"

One sure way *not* to overcome the obstacles to sale is to minimize or dismiss customers' inertia or fear. No. You have to acknowledge it and convince them that buying from you is not as risky as they think. How do you do that?

1. **Try It—You Will Like It.** Let prospects sample the product for free. By sampling it and testing it, they do not have to decide to change until after they know, use, and see the benefits of the product.

2. **Give Away Free Samples.** Have you ever gone in a grocery store or a bakery and tasted a sample of a muffin, cookie, a cooked dish, some cheese, and so on? You were trying a free sample to see if you liked it. Did you ever buy that product? Yes—you did.

3. **Give Demonstrations.** Sometimes it helps to get the buyer and his or her boss together for lunch or after work and give a demonstration of your product—along with a free lunch or snack.

4. **Absolute Happiness Guarantee.** Sometime it takes the "absolute happiness" offer: "If at any time, for any reason you are unhappy, I will give you a 100% money-back guarantee (or even a 105% money-back guarantee)."

5. **Free Repairs/Service for Six Months.** To encourage people to buy, you can offer free repairs or free service for a time period.

6. **Deferred Payment Plans.** Make it easy for your first customers. If applicable, let them pay over time.

7. **References/Testimonials.** The main purpose of your first sales is not money—it is to get good references—testimonials that you can use to make other sales. Remember, no one wants to be the first buyer. The best advertising, the best way to make people comfortable, is to have happy, satisfied customers willing to recommend your business to others.

Business Rule #32:

You need satisfied customers quickly. It is okay to reduce your price to get your first customers.

Business Rule #33:

The hardest sale is the first sale. The second hardest sale is the second sale.

Making Sales Takes Practice

The key to making sales is getting the customer to talk, to tell you his or her needs and to voice concerns and objections. To know or be able to make an educated guess about the selling objections, you have to listen. The hardest thing for enthusiastic sales people to do is to **know when to shut up and listen**. Make the pitch, and if the prospective buyer does not respond, ask him or her questions:

1. Do you think my product will meet your needs?
2. Why not?
3. If not, what are *your* needs?

The Psychology of Sales

There are hundreds of books, courses, seminars, and DVDs on selling techniques. But selling is pretty simple:

- Not all prospects are buyers.
- People buy from nice people—people they can trust.
- It takes time—visits, calls, meetings, and so on to build trust.
- Trust is established by honesty, telling the truth about your product about what it can do and what it cannot do.
- Trust is established because you want to build relationships. The buyer represents more to you than just money.
- Trust is established by admitting mistakes when you make them, fixing them quickly, saying you are sorry, and making the customer happy.
- People want to do business with people they can rely on and who show up on time, do the job well, and are pleasant to be around. These types of relationships take time to build.
- *Never, never* bad-mouth the competition. Win on the merits of your own product or service.

The Customer Buying Timeline

Understanding the customer buying timeline is really about understanding a few things:

- What is the number of people who have to approve the sale?

- When and how often do they meet to make the decisions? Daily, weekly, monthly?
- How badly do they need your product?

Time Is Your Enemy—Your Money Is Burning

Remember that when starting out, you have time pressures. You need to make enough sales right away to stay in business.

Be smart.

Learn to qualify your sales prospects. You need to spend your time on those prospects that appear to be easier to sell. Remember your goal is *quick sales*—sales that will generate references, satisfied customers, and cash.

Selling Is Like Fishing

Every sale requires a hook—just like fishing. What do fly fishers do? Well, they study the facts: water flow, rocks, insects, and temperature and make a choice as to the right fly to throw in the water to catch a fish. They try a fly. If the fish does not bite after three or four passes, what do they do? Well, they try another fly and another fly until they get a strike.

In selling you need different "flies," too. Different flies for you are different reasons for a potential customer to buy your product. If the customer does not strike at your first pitch, change and make another one.

With experience, you will learn that there are two or three key common reasons why people will buy your product.

Keep listening and trying ideas until the prospect bites, and when he or she bites, set the hook. Focus on that point and close the sale by asking him or her to buy for that reason. When you have made the sale, **stop selling and start papering**.

Get the buyer's signature, check, money, and get out of there fast before he changes his mind. Too many people keep talking after they have made the sale. Nothing better can happen. Stop talking, get the money, and leave.

Customer Referral Programs and Customer Loyalty Programs

If you are selling products or services that allow you to do this, select happy customers and make it beneficial for them to refer customers to you and make it beneficial for them to buy more from you.

Reward customers for sending you buyers, not prospects. Reward customers for buying more.

The easiest sale to make is one to a satisfied customer. The second easiest sale to make is to a satisfied customer's family, friend, or business associate. You can reward customer referrals and customer loyalty by gifts or discounts, such as coupons, free dinners, free movie tickets, and so on.

Business Rule #34:
Selling can be learned—it takes practice.

Business Rule #35:
Selling is showing people how your product meets their needs.

Start with a Customer

If at all possible, the best way to start a business is to have customers from the very beginning. How do you do this? This is more likely to occur if you are working in a particular type of business and want to start a similar one because you see an opportunity your current boss does not care about or want to address. Working for someone else lets you learn the business, understand the suppliers, and learn on someone else's money how to sell those products and services. That is how Wal-Mart, Home Depot, and Starbucks were all started. The founders learned the business as employees first.

Remember the business rules:

Business Rule #29:
Selling is overcoming obstacles to a sale.

Business Rule #30:
You cannot listen when you are talking.

Business Rule #31:
You will make few sales convincing buyers you are smarter than they are or that you know their businesses better than they do.

Business Rule #32:
You need satisfied customers quickly. It is okay to reduce your price to get your first customers.

Business Rule #33:
The hardest sale is the first sale. The second hardest sale is the second sale.

Business Rule #34:
Selling can be learned—it takes practice.

Business Rule #35:
Selling is showing people how your product meets their needs.

Chapter Seven: Lessons Learned

1. Customer inertia is real and serious.
2. To make a sale, you need to overcome obstacles to sale.
3. You cannot overcome what you do not understand. You have to ask questions and listen.
4. The sale starts when you understand the reasons why the prospect does not want to buy.
5. There are 9 common reasons people do not buy.
6. There are 7 techniques to get people to try your product.
7. Selling is like fishing—find the right hook.
8. Understand the customer timeline to buy.
9. Reward customer referrals and loyalty.

How to Manage
Your Business

CHAPTER TOPICS

- *Management and start-up overload*
- *Flow charting your value chain, supply chain, and manufacturing chain*
- *Creating processes for quality control and efficiency*
- *Customers' desire for quality on-time delivery and kind service*
- *Management by objectives*
- *Management by exceptions*
- *The power of prioritization and simplicity*
- *The Rule of 3s and the Rule of 7s*
- *Measuring and rewarding employees' performance*
- *Management from the front lines*
- *Iteration—the necessity of improving every day*
- *Creating a positive working atmosphere for employees*

> **Business Rule #36:**
> Management is teaching, motivating, and rewarding others for doing their jobs how you want, when you want, and at the speed you want.

Management is also the coordination of people, supplies, and other inputs that together allow you to make your product *on time* and *defect-free—**every time**.*

Start-Up Overload

Let's assume you have started a business and you have made some sales and you have satisfied customers—congratulations! What now?

You are responsible for everything from turning on the lights, ordering supplies, making product, seeking new customers, hiring help, sweeping the floor, and paying the bills to being a good family person and getting enough sleep. Welcome to *start-up overload.* But, surprisingly, you are energized, motivated, and having fun.

What we want to focus on in this chapter is how you keep control of all the moving parts and in essence manage yourself, prioritizing your time so that you can take care of the critical tasks necessary for your success every day.

You will learn that feeling overwhelmed, having too much to do, and never catching up is normal and does not go away. You will also learn to tell the difference between must-dos and nice-to-dos *real* fast. To do this you need a way of understanding your business as a linked chain of processes. This linked chain is your *value chain.*

Your Value Chain

Your value chain is composed of all the components, the parts, and the building blocks of your business. A value chain represents each step necessary to make and sell your product or service (see Figure 8.1).

Flow charting your value chain is important for two reasons:

1. It makes you more aware of all the steps necessary to make and deliver your product or service.

2. It shows you how many different instructional manuals (your processes) you ultimately need to create— in other words, your cookbook or instruction manual so that others (employees) can do the steps as you would do them, consistently and at a high quality.

The key parts of your value chain are

- Your *inputs* (supplies-ingredients) that go into the product or service creation or manufacturing process.

- What you do with the inputs to make the product.

- How do you deliver the product to the customer?

- How you service customers (help them)?

- How do you keep count of your costs and revenue—your accounting, billing, and collection process?

- How do you know that your customer is happy or satisfied?

- How do you find new customers?

- How do you keep up with what your competition is doing?

- How do you control and manage your cash flow?

- How do you know you are producing quality, defect-free products on time?

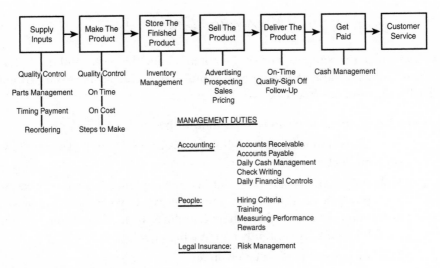

Figure 8.1 *Value chain*

Your Supply Chain

One of your greatest challenges is that you must manage and work on different parts of the chain every day—and you have to deal with some of them simultaneously. As you grow, you'll see that all of this stuff happens every day.

Your supply chain includes all the ingredients that you need to deliver a finished, high-quality product to your customer.

- What are the key parts, supplies, or components that you will need to make your product?
- Where can you buy them?
- At what price?
- When and on what basis do you have to pay for those supplies?

KEY POINT:

Will your inputs supplier allow you to pay him after your customer pays you?

Your Manufacturing (Assembling) Chain

Your manufacturing, assembling, or creation process is composed of each step-by-step item you need to do with or to your inputs (raw materials) to make what you are selling. Let's take an example: baking a cake (see Table 8.1).

Table 8.1 *Manufacturing Chain Example: Baking a Cake*

Inputs/Supplies +	Equipment/Utensils +	Delivery Material	
Butter	Spatulas	Box	
Flour	Mixer	Wrapping	
Flavoring	Bowls	Ribbon	
Yeast	Baking Pans	Logo	= Cake
Baking Soda	Soap and Water	Carrying Bag	
Nuts	Brushes	Customer Instructions	
Chocolate	Oven	Freshness Protection	
Cherries	Electricity or Gas		
	Oven Mittens		

The purpose of the manufacturing chain is to illuminate all the details—the steps you need to undertake and all the parts and supplies you need to do the job. Managing the business is the process of *"changing inputs into outputs."*

We left out a key component in our cake example—didn't we?

Yes, we also must include the step-by-step instructions for *how to make the cake* (see Figure 8.2). These instructions have to be written down clearly enough that an employee who does not know how to make a cake could understand and follow them. This will be your manual, so you have to write it in a simple form so that anyone can follow it.

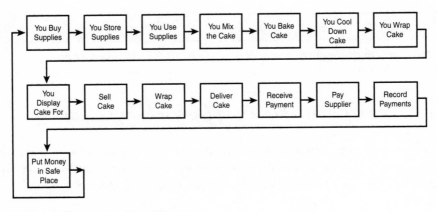

Figure 8.2   *Baking a cake: key processes*

Each of the steps in Figure 8.2 must be drilled down into to create granular cookbook processes detailing how to do each step. That is *Execution Process*. Remember, you cannot get too granular.

Why Do You Flow Chart Your Business?

Each step along the value chain is something you have to

- Focus on daily
- Manage daily
- Improve daily

Value chains help you drill down to the details of execution—the *how* you will get it done.

Horst Schulte, the former CEO of Ritz Carlton Hotels, used to teach Ed's entrepreneurship classes for one hour. Horst told the students he could teach them in that hour everything they needed to know about building a successful business, as shown in Business Rule #37.

> **Business Rule #37:**
>
> The Horst Schulte Rule: No matter what the business is, customers want the same three things:
>
> 1. A defect-free, quality product
> 2. On-time delivery
> 3. To be treated nicely

Defect-free and on-time delivery requires you to create *processes* (ways of doing things that produce good, quality results every time).

Processes are the steps or the instructions you write out, which any employee can use to do the job like you would do it. These steps or instructions should be improved upon by employees and updated as your business grows and develops. Your employees ultimately should take on the ownership of their jobs and their processes and become better and faster each day.

So you have to focus first on the key steps and then write down instructions to be followed by others. By doing this first, you are creating a process:

Process	=	Standardization
	=	Details of Execution
	=	Quality

Management by Objectives

You are starting a business. Every day there are hundreds of things you need to do—find customers, serve customers, make products, buy supplies, keep customers happy, keep up with the money, train employees, oversee employees, motivate employees, and so on. How do you manage? How do you keep control and prioritize your tasks?

You manage by objectives. Objectives are goals—"to-dos." You will have long-term, short-term, and daily goals and objectives.

Each day before the start of the day you should write down your objectives for that day. Then at lunchtime, you should evaluate them based on your morning experience and then write down your afternoon objectives. Management by objectives helps you *prioritize and focus* your time on the most critical important tasks. It helps you spend your time on the important stuff and helps you not be overwhelmed everyday by minutia. Management is a daily prioritization and focus exercise. What are your most important goals?

- Making high-quality products
- Supplying products on time
- Producing satisfied customers
- Managing cash and expenses

You manage by objectives or goals day-in, day-out, no excuses, no exceptions. You set goals, and you achieve them. Then you set new goals.

Business Rule #38:

Business is like farming: You get up every day, you till some soil, you plant, you water, you fertilize, you pull weeds, you harvest, and you get up and do it again tomorrow and the next day, and the next day....

Business Rule #39:

Business is not complex; it is pretty simple. Make and sell something that someone needs. And do it defect-free, on time, with great service. Business is the details—the little things all added together that drive success. You need to focus on the details of execution.

> **Business Rule #40:**
> You are only as good as your last sale. Complacency will kill you.

> **Business Rule #41:**
> You build your business one customer at a time.

Management by objectives teaches you to prioritize because all problems and issues do not have equal weight. This is a hard thing for most people to learn. Many people start businesses and fail, unfortunately. All of these people probably worked very hard. But hard work is not enough. You have to work hard on the key stuff—the right stuff. But what is the right stuff?

1. *Finding and serving customers:* Without customers, you are out of business!

2. *Quality and customer satisfaction:* Unless you meet customer needs and deliver a quality product, you're out of business!

3. *Cash flow:* If you do not produce cash in excess of your costs in a reasonable amount of time, you are broke and out of business!

So setting objectives can be as simple as

- Making five calls today on new, qualified sales prospects
- Calling three customers, thanking them, and asking them for more business
- Focusing on getting the two last customer orders shipped ahead of time

You have to follow up and make sure the right things are getting done the right way. Is this hard? Yes. Can you do it? Yes. Why do we say that? Because millions of people—no smarter than you—are doing it every day.

- You manage by doing.
- You manage by knowing what is going on.
- You manage by making sure the priorities are getting done the right way and on time.

Management by objectives is a *prioritization* process that will teach you to automatically focus your limited time on those tasks most important to your business success.

Most people who start their own businesses will tell you they worked harder in it than they did on a job. But most will also tell you they loved it. They were the bosses. They had the power and worked to do the job right and to make the customers happy as they saw fit.

You, as an owner/manager of a small business, can learn a lot from how the military trains its squad leaders. They are taught to

- Assess the situation.
- Determine what needs to be done.
- Ask how they can have the impact.
- Do it.
- Evaluate/Learn/Improve.
- Move on to the next problem.

Management by Exceptions

You go to your business today. A lot is going on. You have your daily objectives, which are prioritized to make you and your employees focus on what is really important. You have had your daily morning team-teaching meeting.

Guess what? Stuff happens.

Something will always go wrong. Managing by exceptions is managing and fixing what goes wrong.

> **Business Rule #42:**
> All businesses will make mistakes. Mistakes are a given.

Your objectives in managing by exception should be to

- Know or find out about the mistakes quickly
- Fix the mistakes
- Learn and do not make the same mistakes again

Employees are human beings. Human beings make mistakes. Accept that.

OUTBACK STEAKHOUSE RULE:

Teach; don't punish.

How can you find out about the mistakes? You might see it, your customer could complain, or your employees can catch the mistakes for you.

> **Business Rule #43:**
> You cannot fix mistakes, and you cannot limit the damage unless you know about mistakes. Reward mistake illumination and do not "shoot" the messenger.

Common mistakes are

- *Waste*: Supplies are wasted, stolen, or lost, resulting in higher costs and lowering profits.
- *Theft*: Cash is stolen because someone other than the owner can write checks or count the cash daily.
- *Poor quality:* Sloppiness.
- *Late deliveries*

- *Treating customers badly*: Being short, rude, uncaring, or not giving them all your attention.
- *Poor cash management*: Not managing costs, receivables, and the checkbook.
- *Over-promising to customers*: Only promise what you can do.
- *Lying about what you sell and what you can deliver*: The truth always comes out.
- *Trying to cover up mistakes*: Mistakes will happen—admit them and make them right.
- *Violating the Golden Rule*: The essence of dealing with employees and customers.

The Power of Simplicity

The military's "KISS" principle works: **K**eep **I**t **S**imple, **S**tupid.

It is far better to do a few things excellently than to be a master of none.

Businesses are built like houses. First, you need the right foundation. Then you add the sides and roof. All of these basics are time-consuming. But you have to get the basics right, or the house will fall down. Only after you have a firm foundation do you worry about the bells and whistles (curtains and furnishings). You want to build a business in the same way.

You have a dream. You can see the end game—a thriving business with 25 employees and two locations, you making good money, and even driving a new company car every three years. Dreams are good. They are your long-term goals. But what do you have to do first today to achieve your dreams?

Meet a Customer's Need Better, Faster, or Cheaper Than the Competition.

Each day is a new game. What counts is your performance today—not yesterday. Go in each day with the right attitude.

> **Business Rule #44:**
> Every day is *Show Time!*

And to stay a winner, you have to get better. Getting better means improving, and you improve in small steps (incrementally).

Do not try to make big changes all the time—make small steps. Why? Eventually, you will have employees, and employees as people can only learn so fast and can only accommodate or accept so much change. Keeping it simple has many positive results:

- You focus on what is important.
- You can teach people in a digestible fashion.
- You can drill down to processes more easily and then work daily to *tweak* and incrementally improve how you do the key stuff.

"Keep it simple, stupid" also teaches us the *Rule of 3s* and the *Rule of 7s*.

Rule of 3s

Most people can focus on no more than three key things at any one time. Do not overwhelm employees or customers with long lists. What are the three key things people need to learn or do today?

- Can you, in a short, concise, and clear sentence or two, explain to someone what your business is?
- Can you explain how you are different or better than the competition in a short sentence?
- Can you explain to every employee why his or her specific job is important?
- Can you explain to every employee the three things he or she must do everyday?
- Can you explain to each employee how he will be graded and rewarded?

- Can you explain in a short sentence to each employee what three things are *not* under any circumstances allowable behavior?

Business Rule #45:

The George Bernard Shaw Rule:

- Tell them what you are going to tell them.
- Tell them.
- Tell them what you just told them.

Business Rule #46:

Jack Welch, former GE CEO: "You cannot communicate too much."

Rule of 7s

Most people can only manage seven or fewer people at a given time. So as you grow your business and increase the number of employees, you will need to add *structure*—a shift manager or an assistant manager who has responsibility to help manage employees. The Rule of 7 comes from the military, as did KISS.

Measurements and Rewards

If you will have other people (employees) working for you, there are two fundamental management principles you must understand, as listed in Business Rule #47.

Business Rule #47:

1. People are likely to do what you want when you *measure* that performance.
2. People are more likely to do what you want if you measure it *and* reward those behaviors.

Measurements are how you keep score. For example, you have started a new business, and like all new businesses, you need paying customers to make profits. So you hire a salesperson. How will you measure her performance?

- Number of sales calls each day?
- Number of sales calls on qualified prospects?
- Number of sales made per week?
- Number of satisfied customers?
- Number of profitable sales?
- Number of profitable cash sales?

You can see that you have many alternatives, and you should choose the key measures. Measure the desired behaviors and think about the results you want. Many people fail to *drill down* to think about what is really important.

- Is it the number of sales calls, or is it the number of sales calls on *qualified (likely)* buyers?
- Is it the number of sales made, or is it the number of *profitable* sales made?
- Is it sales made or satisfied customers?

People will do what you measure.

Now you have to be fair. You should measure what employees are responsible for and what they can "control." If you measure number of sales, and you created a product no one wants—that is your fault, not theirs.

If you want 25 sales calls a day by phone or 5 sales visits a day, you will get that. But you may find a low percentage hit rate or conversion rate. That is, someone may have to make many, many calls before you get a sale.

Okay, so you decide to measure qualified sales calls—calling on five solid, pre-qualified prospects (likely buyers) a day. Better. But are you paying them to generate prospects or sales? If prospects, then who closes the sale? You? What do you truly want?

Profitable Sales

with

Satisfied Customers

who

Pay on Time

If a salesperson promises extras to make a sale, will the sale still be profitable? If to beat the competition, the salesperson over-promises or represents the product inaccurately, will you have a very satisfied customer? **NO**.

So as you can see, we are pushing you to think through what you measure and how you reward it. When should you reward the salesperson?

Time of Sale?

Time of Delivery?

Time of Payment?

It depends on your view of his job. Will he be responsible for the customer in after-sale service and customer satisfaction? Will the salesperson be the lead contact with the customer, or will you?

What if the salesperson leaves? If you do not know the customer well, is the customer going to stay with you or follow the salesperson?

TIP:

All salespeople should sign an agreement stating all customers are owned by the business and they agree not to solicit or take customers to a competitor for a set time period and within a set geographical area.

The other thing we know about motivation and reward is that *rewards closely linked in time to good behaviors produce more good behaviors.* So bonuses or sales commissions need to be paid often in close time proximity to the behavior. The same rule applies for "penalties" regarding bad behavior.

Measurements also work better if they are

- Transparent
- Objective
- Fairly applied
- Rarely changed

We cannot tell you the absurd number of business owners who change sales compensation programs because salespeople are making too much money. Huh?

If you are measuring the right stuff, you should be making a lot of money if a salesperson is making a lot of money. Why would you reduce or change the compensation plan or cut geography down so salespeople will make less? Excuse me. Why not just put a gun to your head?

The other thing we know about high performance businesses is that they keep "the rules of the game" (how employees are measured and rewarded) relatively stable over a long period of time. This builds trust with employees that if they play by your rules and perform, they will be treated fairly, consistently, and have the opportunity to advance.

Never Change:

Your values

Your standards

Your key policies

Always Change:

Job execution to be better and faster

Stay on the Front Lines

Sam Walton used to say he followed the "management by walking around" principle. He was right. Good managers are on the front lines with employees and customers. And good managers do not hide in their offices or yearn for a nice office with a secretary guarding the door. Good managers are on the front lines seeing, learning, motivating, and leading by example.

Because we know that the goal in any business is to constantly improve and be better each day, you as the owner have to know what is going on and constantly teach and inspire.

> **Business Rule #48:**
> Employees will act toward customers as you act toward employees. *Employees will imitate you.*

Employees in this regard are like young people. They model themselves after role models. If you want employees to be nice to your customers and say thank you, you have to treat your employees with respect, dignity, and say thank you to them.

Constant, be-better environments are created by engaged, involved managers (leaders) who follow the Golden Rule, lead by example, and who do what is right.

By definition, this kind of constant improvement environment requires an atmosphere where mistakes are accepted so they are corrected and learned from. Mistakes are teaching opportunities, not punishment opportunities.

Iteration

Iteration is the taking of small steps to be better. Many small improvements add up to a competitive advantage. In fact, what makes great companies better than the competition is the fact that they constantly improve. Iteration is the process of becoming better and faster. Your customers and employees will tell you what to improve if you ask and listen.

Make Work Fun

Your goal is to do a lot of business and to generate sizable income. To do this you will likely need employees, and you are dependent on them for your income. Like it or not—you need them.

To make money, you need to sell a lot of products that are high quality. High quality comes from processes that produce standardization, which comes from repetition: doing the task the same way every day. Repetition becomes boring. That is why you have to throw in some fun sometime. Some breaks, some ice cream, some pizza. Give people some paid time off and play games, hold contests, celebrate birthdays, and so on. You want to create an atmosphere in which making you money is more than a job for your employees.

Remember: You started your own business because you did not like being an employee. So manage your work environment to have fun sometimes. Make being your employee fun and meaningful.

And remember the business rules:

Business Rule #36:
Management is teaching, motivating, and rewarding others for doing their jobs how you want, when you want, and at the speed you want.

Business Rule #37:
The Horst Schulte Rule: No matter what the business is, customers want the same three things:
1. A defect-free, quality product
2. On-time delivery
3. To be treated nicely

Business Rule #38:
Business is like farming: You get up every day, you till some soil, you plant, you water, you fertilize, you pull weeds, you harvest, and you get up and do it again tomorrow, and the next day, and the next day....

Business Rule #39:
Business is not complex; it is pretty simple. Make and sell something that someone needs. And do it defect-free, on time, with great service.
Business is the details—the little things all added together that drive success. You need to focus on the details of execution.

Business Rule #40:
You are only as good as your last sale. Complacency will kill you.

Business Rule #41:
You build your business one customer at a time.

Business Rule #42:
All businesses will make mistakes. Mistakes are a given.

Business Rule #43:
You cannot fix mistakes, and you cannot limit the damage unless you know about mistakes. Reward mistake illumination and do not "shoot" the messenger.

Business Rule #44:
Every day is Show Time!

Business Rule #45:
The George Bernard Shaw Rule:
- Tell them what you are going to tell them.
- Tell them.
- Tell them what you just told them.

Business Rule #46:
Jack Welch, former GE CEO: "You cannot communicate too much."

Business Rule #47:
1. People are likely to do what you want when you *measure* that performance.
2. People are more likely to do what you want if you measure it *and* reward those behaviors.

Business Rule #48:
Employees will act toward customers as you act toward employees. Employees will imitate you.

Chapter Eight: Lessons Learned

1. Management is the daily focus on producing high-quality products on time that meet customer needs, and it is the coordination of supplies, parts, processes, and people to get that desired result.

2. Every business has a value chain that should focus you on the parts of the business you need to manage.

3. You need to develop value chain as well as supply chain and manufacturing chain flow charts.

4. Management's goal is to get the same high-quality result 99% of the time.

5. Management achieves 99% high-quality results through processes—drilling each job down to each step needed to complete it well.

6. Employees not only have to learn the job but also have to get better and faster; they have to constantly improve.

7. Good managers manage daily by objectives—the prioritized to-dos.

8. Good managers teach at least 15 minutes everyday to all employees the key objectives, the "have-to-dos" to be successful and the "cannot-dos."

9. Managing by exception is how you focus on the mistakes and problems.

10. Mistakes are a given. The key is to find them out quickly and fix them before they become big mistakes.

11. KISS: Keep It Simple, Stupid.

12. Learn to communicate clearly, concisely, and compellingly.

13. Constant improvement is far more important than doing it right the first time.

14. Structure becomes necessary when you have more than seven employees.

15. Measuring employees' performance is critical.

16. Measure the right things. Measure behaviors that create the right results.

17. Measure frequently and give results to all employees.

18. Reward what you measure.

19. Make work fun; make work a game to learn.

20. Create a constant improvement business, a high-performance environment.

21. High-performance environments are positive, energetic places to work and are based on the Golden Rule.

22. You need the committed hearts and minds of your employees to make money.

chapter nine

How Do You Find and Keep Good Employees?

CHAPTER TOPICS

- *People will be a big challenge.*
- *What employees want.*
- *Hiring for fit: focusing on values, drive, and motivation. Hire people who want to work hard to get ahead.*
- *Doing your research when hiring—asking questions, checking references, and hiring everyone on a trial basis.*
- *Creating a positive atmosphere for your employees.*
- *The importance of employee buy-in and playing to people's strengths.*
- *Instructing and training your employees and promoting from within.*
- *Setting clear expectations of both desirable and undesirable behaviors.*
- *Managing best practices:*
  - *Treating your employees well and creating a "family" atmosphere.*
  - *Hiring people like your customers.*
  - *Creating meaning for your employees.*
  - *Leading by example.*
- *Managing you!*

We truly hope you need to read this chapter because it means that either you can afford employees or your business has more work than you and your family can do alone.

This People Stuff Is Hard

This people stuff is hard because people are human beings with faults and emotions. It takes hard work to learn how to hire, how to train, and how to inspire and motivate people to work hard to make *your* business a success.

High-performance organizations have learned that people will work harder if they feel part of something that they can be proud of. Create an environment where your employees feel part of a team and a "family" at work.

A "family-at-work" feeling comes about because the leaders care about their employees as people, not just as "horses pulling a wagon" or a "cog in the wheel."

The #1 challenge to growing a business is—**people**.

Business Rule #49:

Happy Employees +
Happy Customers =
You make money

And

Happy Employees = Higher
Productivity, Higher Quality,
and Higher Loyalty

Business Rule #50:

Boss + Happy Employee =
Happy Customer

Or

Boss + Unhappy Employee =
Unhappy Customer

How you treat your employees will determine whether or not they will help you make money.

What Do Employees Want?

Employees want the same things you want. They want to be treated
- With respect
- With dignity
- Honestly
- Fairly

Employees also want to have the opportunity to learn and advance and as the U.S. Army says, "Be all you can be." And being listened to and having some say over their lives is necessary for employees to fully buy-in to your program.

Why Is High Employee Turnover Bad?

Neither you nor we are good enough or smart enough to hire the right people all the time. But employee turnover is costly, disruptive, and takes your eye "off the ball"—satisfied, paying customers. It is frustrating and time-consuming hiring people, getting them trained correctly, and then having to start all over with a new employee after the experienced good employee leaves. Quality and efficiency suffers with constant employee turnover.

Ed, at one point, built a business with 25 employees, and he thought he was good at recognizing "winners"—but numbers do not lie. His hiring success rate was only 50%: Half of the time he was right, and the other half of the time he was wrong.

So he decided he needed to learn hiring best practices—and he did.

So, to avoid the costs, inefficiencies, and resulting customer unhappiness from constant employee turnover, you need to focus on how to avoid the problem—that starts with hiring the right people.

Hire for Fit

Most successful business builders have learned that it is better to hire for cultural fit—focusing on values fit over just hiring for skills.

Hire people with the right attitude and a track record of success. Hire people with high standards with integrity. Hire people with the drive to work hard and the drive to succeed to make a better life for themselves and their families.

One big company that Ed researched learned after 15 years of hiring that they simply should hire the "glass is half full" people and not "the glass is half empty" people.

That is a pretty good summary because how one approaches life or the day is really critical. Customers and other employees want to be around positive people—people who cast light, not darkness.

Other lessons to be learned about hiring are

1. Men and women with military service or training have been taught the value of rules, hard work, teamwork, process and thus can make good employees.

2. People who have experienced and rebounded successfully from adversity have character. Look for someone wanting to make his or her life better. Think about it—work is the means or avenue through which most people try to achieve their dreams for themselves and their families. Find people who want to join your journey and when you find them, take care of them.

3. Hire people like your customers. Sam Walton built Wal-Mart by hiring people just like his customers—people from small towns who understood the value of a dollar and who came from humble backgrounds. Employees who are like your customers can relate easier to and better understand your customers.

Hiring Tools

To increase your chances of success, interview people two or three times. Check their backgrounds and work references. Ask references direct, blunt questions and listen to how they answer. Listen to the tone or how fast or slowly they answer. Listen for them hedging their answers or being hesitant.

Ask job applicants if they have anything embarrassing in their backgrounds. Everyone does, so listen to how they respond. Then decide whether it is important or not to your decision. Ask them if they have ever been charged with a crime and follow up with a background check.

In today's world of lawsuits, references rarely speak directly about negative stuff—they speak indirectly. Ask those providing references if they would have any reservations about hiring the person again. Ask them if they would recommend the person without qualifications, and ask them what the person's weaknesses are. You might not get as detailed information as you would like, but you should always ask.

Probationary Hiring

Hire everybody on a one-month probationary basis. That means you will determine in one month or less whether they have a job. This gives you time to evaluate and test them out. It generally will not take you a month to decide, but it does help protect you if you have made a wrong choice.

Buy-In

The ultimate question is: Will the employee "buy-in" and find meaning in working for your business? Will doing a good job be meaningful? Do they see the purpose of what you are trying to do? If you are starting a bakery that offers cakes and cookies, for example, you should not hire someone who does not like sweets. How can someone who does not eat dessert passionately make or sell desserts?

If you are doing shoe repair, look at the interviewee's shoes—are they shined? Cared for? Clean?

If you are going to open a home cleaning service, is the interviewee wearing clean, pressed clothes? Do they take pride in their appearance?

So you should

- Hire for fit and willingness to work hard to succeed.
- Hire based on track record.
- Hire ex-military people.
- Hire people who are like your customers.
- Hire people who can relate to your business.
- Hire "the glass is half full" people.
- Hire people who need (not just want) a job.

The Rules of the Game

Employees will need to be taught what to do and how to do it, but they will make mistakes. That is your job is to train them. No one in the beginning is going to do the job as well as you can or would. But your goal is to move employees in that direction.

Teaching and training requires you to take the time to

- Point out mistakes.
- Teach people what to do.
- Give them the opportunity to do it.

If you have hired people of honesty, drive, and willingness to work hard to be successful, find them the right job that plays to their strengths.

> **Business Rule #51:**
> Play to people's strengths. You do not have the time or money to correct people's weaknesses.

Nonetheless, if a person steals, comes to work habitually late or drunk, or becomes physically or verbally abusive with a customer or fellow worker, fire them quickly and on the spot. You and your business must have a ***zero tolerance*** for behavior that is unethical, dishonest, or abusive.

Tell your employees not only what behaviors are good but equally as important, tell people directly and in writing what behaviors will not be tolerated and are grounds for instant dismissal.

Best Practices of Managing Employees

Constant communication and feedback are critical. Here are some keys:

- Explain the job.
- Teach the job.

- Give people the tools to do the job.
- Evaluate often and give feedback frequently.
- Document the feedback.
- If someone is doing something wrong, show him how to do it right.
- Reward good behavior with emotional rewards, too—praise, recognition, and so on.

Elementary grade school teachers are smarter than most managers. They understand the power of "stars"—giving out stars for good performance. You can create a great working atmosphere by

- Saying "thank you."
- Getting to know your people and their lives. In times of personal stress, cut people some slack.
- Asking them monthly whether they are happy in their jobs. If they're not, find out why. Decide whether you can make their jobs better.
- Making work fun and celebrating successes with pizza, ice cream, or a small gift.
- Thinking about work uniforms being a source of pride—shirts and blouses, hats, and bags that builds spirit de corps.

Learn and teach that the most important

- Business *word* is: Improvement.
- Business *phrase* is: Thank you.
- Business *objective* is: Serve your customer.
- Business *question to customers* is: How may I help you?

Promote from Within

As much as you can, promote from within. People want the chance for advancement and "to be all they can be." Great companies such as UPS, SYSCO, Best Buy, Walgreens, and Southwest Airlines have found success in doing this.

The Meaning of Work

Are your employees only a means to your end? Or are your employees the end?

What do we mean by that? If you focus on what your *duty* is to your employees—what you owe them for helping make you successful—you will have a higher chance of success than if you treat your employees like fungible commodities to be used like work horses.

People want and need more than a paycheck. Money by itself is not enough for consistent high performance. People spend a lot of time at work. Create an environment that enables high performance, enthusiasm, and positivity. Emotional recognition and praise are important to people.

Create an environment in which people are proud to work. Constantly explain how your business is helping people or is doing something good.

Also create an atmosphere of being the best at what you do and out-competing the competition. Teach the value and inner joy of excellence and the joy of satisfaction knowing you did your best.

Jimmy Blanchard, the former CEO of Synovus Financial, said he spent a million dollars on consultants trying to learn how to create a high-performance company, and he found out the simple truth:

"Just take care of your people."

Read about great teams like the San Antonio Spurs, the United States Marine Corps, Starbucks, Walgreens, Southwest Airlines, Synovus Financial, UPS, and Best Buy, where employees have become a key driver of success. These companies became great because of their people.

Remember: Happy Employees + Happy Customers = You make money.

The people stuff is all about leadership. There are thousands of leadership books you could read, but leadership is really pretty simple:

1. Take care of your people.
2. Live the Golden Rule.
3. Lead by example.
4. Never ask anyone to do anything you are not willing to do.

> **Business Rule #52:**
> Before you can manage others, you need to *manage yourself.*

What do we mean? Each day before you go to work, you have to get yourself ready to be enthusiastic and engaged about your business—it is show time. Every day is game day in our world. Go into work with the right attitude—be up, be positive, be prepared.

Your emotional attitude (good or bad) will infect your workplace and your employees. Prepare yourself to lead by example.

Mental Rehearsal

Each day work out on paper what you want to focus on—what points to teach and what objectives you want to accomplish.

Think ahead of time what you need to do, how you want to do it, and how you will handle surprises, mistakes, or problems. Think about your employees—who needs encouragement or who needs teaching. Think about your customers—who needs to hear from you. Think about all aspects of your business before the day starts.

Prepare, prepare, prepare.

Mental Replay

After each day replay in your head the events of the day—what went right? What went wrong? What could you have done better? What process needs to be improved? What mistakes need to be corrected?

Mental replay is how you learn. Each day you should be determined to do at least one thing better than you did yesterday. Infuse your employees with that goal:

"Let's be better today than we were yesterday."

And remember:

Business Rule #49:

Happy Employees + Happy Customers = You make money
And
Happy Employees = Higher Productivity, Higher Quality, and Higher
Loyalty

Business Rule #50:

Boss + Happy Employee = Happy Customer
Or
Boss + Unhappy Employee = Unhappy Customer

Business Rule #51:

Play to people's strengths. You do not have the time or
money to correct people's weaknesses.

Business Rule #52:

Before you can manage others, you need to manage yourself.

Chapter Nine: Lessons Learned

1. Employees are people, too. They want the same exact things you want—dignity, respect, and the opportunity to be all they can be.

2. Hire for *fit*; focus on values and character. You can teach skills—you cannot teach character and drive.

3. Become good at hiring. Hire only after a thorough investigation and a probationary period. Hire people with a track record of success.

4. Hire employees who are like your customers. They will understand and relate to your customers better.

5. Play to people's strengths. You do not have enough time to fix people's weaknesses.

6. Be clear about what the job is. Be truthful and manage expectations.

7. Teach—Teach—Teach.

8. Inform your employees often what behaviors are *not* tolerated. Give daily/weekly feedback and keep records.

9. Be fair, consistent, and honest. Lead by example.

10. Ask your employees monthly if they are happy. If they aren't, why not? Happy employees result in happy customers. How you treat your

employees is the critical determination of whether they are happy and how they will perform.

11. Make work fun and meaningful, and when you can, always promote from within.

12. High-performance organizations create a "family."

13. Remember: Happy Employees + Happy Customers = You make money.

14. Take care of your people.

15. Manage yourself as thoroughly as you manage your employees. Mentally rehearse the day to come and mentally replay the previous day to see where you can make improvement.

chapter ten

How Do You Manage Growth?

CHAPTER TOPICS

- *Growth can be good or bad*
- *Growth will stretch your resources*
- *Growth requires more employees and more cash*
- *To manage growth you have to maintain high quality standards*
- *To maintain high quality you will need a hiring and training process*
- *Manage the unexpected*
- *Use of outsourcing or part-timers*
- *Legal contracts and structure*
- *Upgrading employees*
- *Customer diversification*
- *Growth changes your job*

Most businesses face the same two major inflection points at which failure rates can be high:

1. Start-up survival—getting past break-even to making money
2. Managing growth

Building a successful business is challenging, fun, rewarding, scary, and just plain hard work, and you must be vigilant at these two points to overcome the potential for failure.

We have spent the first nine chapters focusing on how to avoid the common mistakes start-ups make, which is the main focus of this book. We now want to introduce you to the challenges that you will face when you enter a high-growth phase.

Growth Can Be Good or Bad

High growth requires you to manage more business under strong restraints. Those restraints are your limited time and limited money to invest in the business, and too few people to handle the growth. Growth stretches you, your people, and your capabilities. Too much growth too fast makes it hard to maintain quality and timeliness, which every customer wants.

Growth presents you with three big challenges:

1. People
2. Quality
3. Cash

On the people side, you will need more people quickly to serve more customers. Hiring people takes time. Training people takes time. Time is in short supply because you want the new business, need the new business, and are afraid to turn new business away.

So what do you do? First, you have to maintain high quality. That is non-negotiable. **It is better to turn away work than to produce bad work**.

Secondly, you have to ask more of your employees. They will need to work overtime and weekends while you hire and train new employees. Involve your employees in finding new employees and training them.

Likewise with quality. Quality requires more process (instruction manuals) and more checks. You will need to choose your best employees and ask them to help write process instructions, and you will have to create a new structure giving those employees responsibility for oversight, quality control, and checking the work of new employees. This also means that you have to give them a pay raise to reward them for taking on this important role.

Growth will require you to prioritize what you do everyday and will require you to spend more time managing and less time "doing." This is a hard transition for many people because by definition entrepreneurs are doers, not managers.

And let's not forget about ole number one: CASH FLOW. Growth will require you to hire more people, which will increase your weekly payroll. Growth will cause you to have to buy more supplies and raw materials, which are needed by the increasing number of customers, all of which increases your cash payments to others ahead of your receipt of cash from customers.

Managing cash flow becomes even more paramount in a high growth situation because you may have a month lag between increased costs and receipt of cash from customers. How will you manage this?

The first source of that additional cash is you. The second source is a loan from family or friends. The next source of cash is getting your suppliers to finance your purchases of supplies until you deliver the product and collect the cash from customers. Unlikely sources of cash are your new customers and a bank, but it does not hurt to ask. Somehow you have to work through this cash flow timing issue.

Let's make this real. Using our sandwich shop example from Chapter 3, "What Is a Good Business Opportunity?"—you are selling regularly to 50 customers a day at lunch. Because your satisfied customers are spreading the word, all of a sudden you have 100 customers on a Tuesday. Your first thought is "Eureka!" Your second thought is that it is a fluke. But on Wednesday, Thursday, and Friday, you also have in excess of 100 customers.

Thank goodness for the weekend. What do you do? You need more people, more supplies, faster sandwich making, more space, another cash register, and so on because everyone wants high-quality, fast, good service during their lunch hour.

You are now facing the paradox of growth in Business Rule #53.

> **Business Rule #53:**
> Growth can be good if managed well
> Or
> Growth can destroy your business if managed poorly.

The Two Absolutes

When you run the risk of being overrun by growth, what do you do?

First, you have to set your *priorities*:

1. You have to maintain high quality and produce satisfied customers.
2. You have to focus on the money.

Secondly, you "chunk." You break the challenge down into digestible chunks by what is most important, and you do those things first. What do you need to do?

You need more employees. How many? Where can you find them?

Can you or should you bootstrap employees? That is, fill in on a temporary basis with whomever you can lay hands on? Do you have friends, family, or employees' family members that can help out until you hire and train more employees?

Be careful and hire slowly. Remember—quality is #1. New people need to be trained and supervised. It is far better to tell potential customers, "Right now we are at full capacity, but we are expanding—please come back. Give us another chance, and here is a gift card for a free sandwich next week."

So what are your priorities?

- Quality
- Financial controls
- Good people

Process

Every part of your business has a process. Process is the *how* of what you do. It is the granular details of: buying supplies, storing supplies, preparing the sandwich ingredients, having a clean shop, having an attractive place to come and eat, ensuring good sandwiches, having sanitary restrooms, and keeping your sandwich line moving.

Drilling down more, process is about

- Cutting tomatoes
- Washing lettuce
- Spreading mustard
- Wrapping sandwiches
- Making coffee
- Restocking supplies
- Controlling costs, waste
- Greeting customers
- Keeping records of what types of sandwiches are selling
- Preventing spoilage

Processes yield checklists. Checklists are teaching tools. The more process you create early on, the easier it is to teach others when growth occurs.

With your checklists, you can give experienced employees the job of teaching new employees. You need short, one-page checklists for your key processes, which are to be filled out and signed each day (see Table 10.1).

Table 10.1 *Checklists*

Employee Checklist		Public Restroom	
Time Checked In	___	Paper Towels	___
Hands Washed	___	Toilet Paper	___
Hair Net On	___	Door Locks Work	___
Clean Appearance	___	Soap Dispenser	___
No exposed scrapes	___	Mirrors Cleaned	___
Gloves Used	___	Sink Cleaned	___
		Floor Cleaned	___
		Toilet Cleaned	___
		Toilet Sanitizer	___
Perishable Food		**Checked At**	
Refrigerator Temperature	___	10 A.M.	___
Food Checked	___	12 P.M.	___
Food Expiration Dates Checked	___	2 P.M.	___

How you ever seen an experienced airline pilot go through his or her checklist before a flight? It is done each and every time, no matter how much experience the pilot has. Checklists are key.

Financing Growth

What happened today? You sold 100 sandwiches, and you exhausted your supplies of tomatoes, lettuce, turkey, and roast beef. What do you do? You need the ingredients for tomorrow. You must replenish—but how much? Was today a fluke? Or should you buy 200 sandwiches worth of supplies? Or should you buy larger quantities and get a discount?

Be conservative: Do not end up with perishables over the weekend. Make sure you control waste.

Growth requires investment—more machinery, another cash register, more tables, more plates, bigger refrigerators. What do you buy first? Where do you find the money? Do you borrow from family? Do you finance with your seller?

Do you go to a bank? Do you put the purchases on your credit card?

You do whatever is *easy*, *quick*, and *cheap*.

Financial Controls

Unfortunately, too many businesses get hurt by embezzlement and theft. You have to control the cash. You must control ordering supplies, and you count the money and make the bank deposit. And until you get much bigger, you should be the only person allowed to sign checks or spend money.

You also need a process to know each day where you stand financially. What did you sell today by type? Total dollars? What did you spend today? Month to date? As you operate the business, adjust your budget so it is realistic as to your costs.

Managing the Unexpected

You need a contingency plan for major risks. For example, with our sandwich shop, what do you do if

- You do not receive delivery one morning of your food supplies?
- Your refrigerator breaks down?
- You have a fire?
- Half of your employees stay home sick?
- A customer finds a hair in his sandwich?
- Your toilet overruns?
- You are very sick with the flu?
- Your child has an emergency at school?
- The electricity in your store goes out?
- A customer faints?
- An employee cuts himself?

For your contingency plan, you need to have thought through what you would do in each case if one of the listed events occurred. You need emergency phone numbers posted for cases of fire, health emergencies, and accidents. If one of these events happens, you need to be prepared ahead of time.

People

You will also need people processes and people controls as you grow.

First, as you gain experience with employees, pick your best two and do a profile of the perfect employee including background, experience, personality, and attitude. What experiences do you think have contributed to their success?

If you wanted to hire more employees like them, what major things would you look for? Create a checklist of what to look for when you hire. Prioritize what has worked so far and what is important to you.

Second, take those key employees and ask them to write out two checklists for you:

1. Instructions to new employees on what it takes to be successful working at your store, rules of conduct (how to treat customers), and rules of appearance.

2. A step-by-step guide to how to do a particular job right each and every time. Assign new employees the simplest, easiest, non-customer interaction jobs. Do this to test them out. Put your best employees "up front," dealing with customers and ensuring the sandwiches are made correctly.

Third, start keeping records of people interviewed and why they were rejected and also keep performance and attendance records for your current employees. You have to hire and fire for specific reasons, and they cannot be based on race, gender, or age—and you need to be able to prove you are doing this.

Fourth, you need to test employees often for drugs.

Fifth, keep records of hours worked and payroll and all applicable federal and state withholdings. Hire a payroll service to process all this for you.

Sixth, as you grow, you will decide whether you will add employee benefits or bonuses to your program. These programs can be costly. Shop wisely. See if there is a small business co-op in your hometown that you could join that would offer you health insurance on a group basis—cheaper than what you can buy on your own.

Small Business Services

As you grow, you will have to decide when and if to hire a part-time bookkeeper, hire an outside accountant to do your taxes, outsource your payroll, or buy computers for your business.

As you grow, you will need timely, quality information to keep control.

Table 10.2 is a checklist of things to consider:

Table 10.2   *Managing a Small Business*

Payroll	Hire payroll service.
Accounting	Hire a part-time accountant.
Accounts Receivable and Payable	Manage yourself daily and weekly.
Inventory Management	Count and order weekly.
HR Records	You update and document weekly.
Legal and Insurance	Start looking for a good business lawyer. Insurance is critical to your business.

As you grow, you will progress as shown in Table 10.3.

Table 10.3   *Other Controls*

Accounting	Move to part-time CPA, then to CPA doing your taxes, then to CPA doing an annual audit.
Accounts Receivable and Payable	Move from you paying bills and collecting money to your part-time controller doing those tasks, to a full-time controller.
HR Records	You do this in the beginning and then move to a part-time HR assistant helping in this area.
Inventory Management	You do this and then you move to a part-time controller and then to a full-time controller.

You will progress from outsourcing to part-time help to full-time help. As you hire accounting and quality control help, you will want to hire people with experience—people who have experience in business growth.

This point bears repeating: As you grow, hire people who have worked in high-growth businesses and who have made the common mistakes and have already learned how to manage and work in the crazy high-growth environment.

The challenges that high growth will present to you are *not* unique to you. Every business faces similar challenges. So when you hire people, hire those who have already learned how to succeed in this environment. Pay for experience. There is no reason you have to make the same mistakes others have made.

Check-Off

Always have two people sign off on any report—have someone periodically check the report to prevent mistakes, theft, and fraud.

Legal

You will move from using a lawyer to form your business to having legal contracts: better forms for invoices, purchase forms and orders, HR forms, confidentiality agreements, non-compete agreements, lease negotiations, and so on.

As you grow, you will step up the quality of your risk management and spend wisely for protection through insurance.

Legal Structure

When you start a business, you should use a legal form of business that protects your personal assets and home and family from liabilities such as a LLC (limited liability company) or a LLP (limited partnership). You can do this yourself by finding the form under your state government website under the Secretary of State or Corporation and Business Department.

Many small businesses start as sole proprietorships—the entrepreneur is the owner. If the business is doing business under a name like "The Sandwich Shoppe," many states require you to register that name as a "doing business as" name. Also many states will require you to get a business license and pay a business tax or property tax.

> **Business Rule #54:**
> Growth requires more
> - Processes
> - Quality Controls
> - Financial Controls
> - Risk Management
> - Real-Time Information

Let's summarize what we have discussed so far:

- Growth will require you to move from doing everything yourself to hiring others to help you.

- Growth requires more checklists, that is, more "recipes" and lists of how to do things.

- Growth requires you to manage cash flow. When you grow, you will incur more costs—money for people, supplies, and products before you receive customer cash.

- Growth will require you to invest more money or to borrow more money unless you can get financing from your suppliers or cash earlier from customers.

As an example, in the sandwich shop, you could sell a weekly discount card enticing the buyer to purchase five sandwiches for $27 instead of the usual price of $30. If they pay in advance, this will decrease your profits, but it will also quickly provide you cash to buy supplies.

Small Business Networks

Growth will be challenging. But you can learn from other entrepreneurs. Most towns have a Chamber of Commerce or Entrepreneurs Network or a Business Club. Go once a month and meet people and ask their advice (make sure to ask *successful* entrepreneurs).

Always remember that every challenge you will face, someone else has faced that same situation, too.

Upgrading People

The toughest part of growth is the people part. You will need employees with skills and experience working for bigger businesses, and you may have to terminate people who have been with you from the start.

You have to upgrade to more skilled and experienced people. Hopefully, you can manage this by keeping loyal employees, but if not, you have to terminate them honestly and fairly.

This is difficult and hard. But many entrepreneurs will tell you their biggest mistake was not doing this fast enough.

Customer Diversification

As you grow, mostly likely your business will grow with some existing customers. *Beware* if any one customer becomes a big part of your business (20% or more). Understand that this customer is not usually making a long-term commitment to you. Always think about what would happen if you lost that customer. Would you have to terminate good employees? Would you have to lease a smaller space?

Ultimately, you would like for no customer to account for more than 10% of your business. You want to be diversified. In business, stuff happens. Customers can be bought, they can move, and they can go out of business.

Growth Changes Your Job

As you grow, you will not be able to do everything yourself. You will have to move from being a full-time "doer" to managing others and overseeing process and controls as well as *some* doing.

Managers are *teachers*. They create checklists for employees. Managers each day check all the important parts of the business. Managers look at the big picture and allocate their time accordingly among customers, production, teaching, quality control, cash management, and getting more business. You have to think about all these responsibilities and do something each day in each area.

You have to *plan* your day, *prioritize* your work, and *focus* on the key parts to make your business successful. You need your daily checklist. You need to think and plan more—**not** just react.

As you grow, you will add levels of sophistication, and you will start to ask harder questions such as

1. ***Is my growth profitable?***

   Not all customers are profitable. Most businesses will tell you that about 80% of the profits come from 20% of the customers. So understand who they are and serve them well. Also understand which 10% to 20% of your customers are unprofitable or painful to serve. Slowly, replace them.

2. ***Am I the right person to grow the business?***

   Some entrepreneurs do not have the skills or personality to manage a larger business and need help—an experienced operations or financial person. First, you have to be careful and hire someone with a great track record with impeccable integrity and honesty.

   And you have to protect yourself legally with contracts and agreements that he or she will not leave you for a competitor or start a competing business and will not hire or steal employees or customers.

   And never, never—without experience and controls—give those people unilateral power over money or ordering or spending your money.

> **Business Rule #55:**
> You and ONLY YOU control the money.

Hire these people first on a trial basis. Check them out with past employers. It is better to hire someone you know in your community. Be wary of people with many jobs in many different cities.

3. *How big do I want to become? How big do I need to be?*

Some people get caught up in the "high" of growth and continue to grow until their businesses are so big they become something different than what they originally wanted.

Always remember growth can be good, and growth can be bad. You should decide how much growth is good for you.

Every level of growth requires more people, more process, more controls, and more cash management. We are not saying that growth is bad for you. We are saying to approach growth and the size of your business realistically and understand that many businesses fail when they expand geographically to more locations or when they diversify into new products or when owners lose control of the money.

Always be wary of the downside—what can go wrong—and have contingency plans and manage for both success and risk management.

Lastly, growth will change your competition. By that we mean you will face bigger competition that may have more money than you and thus can afford to lower their prices to take away your customers. As you grow and expand, that competition will likely view you as a competitive threat. Before growing, you were too small for them to care or worry about.

Remember:

Business Rule #53:
Growth can be good if managed well
Or
Growth can destroy your business if managed poorly.

Business Rule #54:
Growth requires more
- Processes
- Quality Controls
- Financial Controls
- Risk Management
- Real-Time Information

Business Rule #55:
You and ONLY YOU control the money.

Chapter Ten: Lessons Learned

1. Growth can be good or bad.
2. Growth creates people, quality, and financial issues.
3. Growth requires more controls and processes.
4. Growth requires the entrepreneur to become a manager.
5. Managing is different than doing.
6. Every financial area of your business (supplies, inventory, accounting, cash management, HR, and training employees) will need more process and controls.
7. Controls and processes have to be created real-time as you operate the business.
8. Growth will require you to upgrade your employees.
9. Growth will require you to manage customer concentration risk.
10. Growth will require more legal and insurance costs.
11. Growth will stretch you and will require you to operate differently.
12. Growth will require you to manage more proactively than reactively.
13. Growth will change your competition.

Conclusion

Well, what have we learned? Let's review the Business Rules and Lessons Learned from each chapter in this conclusion.

We hope you have learned valuable tools and concepts that you can use to pursue your dream. Best wishes and enjoy your journey.

—Ed and Charlie

Business Rules

Business Rule #1:

The Jerry McGuire Rule: Follow the Money—Cash is King.

Business Rule #2:

The Peter Drucker Rule: "The sole purpose of business is to serve customers."

Business Rule #3:

Customers know best what they need.

Business Rule #4:

You are looking for a good business opportunity—*not* a good idea.

Business Rule #5:

Every entrepreneur over-estimates the number of customers that will buy and the speed at which they will buy.

Business Rule #6:

Happy employees create happy customers, which creates profits for you!

Business Rule #7:
The 7 Ws

1. What can I sell?
2. To Whom can I sell?
3. Why will customers buy from me?
4. At What price?
5. What are my costs?
6. When will customers buy?
7. What will the competition do?

Business Rule #8:

Low Profit Margin = High Volume

High Profit Margin = Lower Volume

Business Rule #9:

Profits are your goal—sooner rather than later.

Business Rule #10:

Cash flow is your business's lifeblood—it is how you pay your bills.

Business Rule #11:

Control your costs—spend wisely on the right stuff.

Business Rule #12:

Know your burn rate—how soon will you run out of money?

Business Rule #13:

Customers are high-probability prospects who actually buy your product.

Business Rule #14:

Focus on high-probability prospects—*not* just anyone willing to listen.

Business Rule #15:

It is easier to convert top- and high-priority prospects to customers than other prospects.

Business Rule #16:

Learn about your industry. Search the Internet and find a relevant trade association.

Business Rule #17:

If someone buys from one of your competitors, *you lose*, and the competitor wins.

Business Rule #18:

When in doubt, always define your competition broadly, not narrowly.

Business Rule #19:

Attack competitors' weaknesses.

Business Rule #20:

Competitors will respond. Business is like a baseball game—there is always another inning.

Business Rule #21:

Customers buy solutions, so you must constantly assess what customers really want or need and make sure you give them that—*not* what you think they need, nor more than they need because they will not want to pay for anything they do not need.

Business Rule #22:

The goal is to deliver the most value to your customer at a price that is both affordable for your customer and profitable for you.

Business Rule #23:

The key is the value perceived by the customer.

Business Rule #24:

Avoid the Winner's Curse: Do not think you will continue winning forever. Do not become complacent or overconfident.

Business Rule #25:

This is the competitive advantage you are seeking: to offer more value at an affordable price and do it defect-free, on time, and with good service every time.

Business Rule #26:

Don't fall in love with your product or service. Be willing to listen to negative feedback and change.

Business Rule #27:

Rarely is it the product or service that is the reason for success in a new business. In reality, it is the execution of the business that is the primary driver of a new venture's success.

Business Rule #28:

Get good customer references as soon as you can. Use them to sell to other customers.

Business Rule #29:

Selling is overcoming obstacles to a sale.

Business Rule #30:

You cannot listen when you are talking.

Business Rule #31:

You will make few sales convincing buyers you are smarter than they are or that you know their businesses better than they do.

Business Rule #32:

You need satisfied customers quickly. It is okay to reduce your price to get your first customers.

Business Rule #33:

The hardest sale is the first sale. The second hardest sale is the second sale.

Business Rule #34:

Selling can be learned—it takes practice.

Business Rule #35:

Selling is showing people how your product meets their needs.

Business Rule #36:

Management is teaching, motivating, and rewarding others for doing their jobs how you want, when you want, and at the speed you want.

Business Rule #37:

The Horst Schulte Rule: No matter what the business is, customers want the same three things:

1. A defect-free, quality product
2. On-time delivery
3. To be treated nicely

Business Rule #38:

Business is like farming: You get up every day, you till some soil, you plant, you water, you fertilize, you pull weeds, you harvest, and you get up and do it again tomorrow, and the next day, and the next day....

Business Rule #39:

Business is not complex; it is pretty simple. Make and sell something that someone needs. And do it defect-free, on time, with great service. Business is the details—the little things all added together that drive success. You need to focus on the details of execution.

Business Rule #40:

You are only as good as your last sale. Complacency will kill you.

Business Rule #41:

You build your business one customer at a time.

Business Rule #42:

All businesses will make mistakes. Mistakes are a given.

Business Rule #43:

You cannot fix mistakes, and you cannot limit the damage unless you know about mistakes. Reward mistake illumination and do not "shoot" the messenger.

Business Rule #44:

Every day is *Show Time!*

Business Rule #45:

The George Bernard Shaw Rule:

- Tell them what you are going to tell them.
- Tell them.
- Tell them what you just told them.

Business Rule #46:

Jack Welch, former GE CEO: "You cannot communicate too much."

Business Rule #47:

1. People are likely to do what you want when you *measure* that performance.

2. People are more likely to do what you want if you measure it *and* reward those behaviors.

Business Rule #48:

Employees will act toward customers as you act toward employees. *Employees will imitate you.*

Business Rule #49:

Happy Employees +
Happy Customers =
You make money

And

Happy Employees = Higher Productivity, Higher Quality, and Higher Loyalty

Business Rule #50:

Boss + Happy Employee =
Happy Customer

Or

Boss + Unhappy Employee =
Unhappy Customer

Business Rule #51:

Play to people's strengths. You do not have the time or money to correct people's weaknesses.

Business Rule #52:

Before you can manage others, you need to *manage yourself.*

Business Rule #53:

Growth can be good if managed well

Or

Growth can destroy your business if managed poorly.

Business Rule #54:

Growth requires more
- Processes
- Quality Controls
- Financial Controls
- Risk Management
- Real-Time Information

Business Rule #55:

You and ONLY YOU control the money.

Lessons Learned

Chapter One

1. Businesses succeed only by meeting customer needs.

2. Businesses succeed because they make profits.

3. Business profit equals cash in from customer minus cash out for costs.

4. Successful entrepreneurs meet customers' needs better, faster, or cheaper than someone else.

5. IQ, education, family background, race, religion, and ethnic origin are not predictive of entrepreneurial success.

6. Successful serial entrepreneurs are not big risk takers—they take small-measured risks.

7. Most successful entrepreneurs are not inventors or discoverers or geniuses.

8. Business is about people. You need people to buy your product, people to work hard for you, and people to finance your business.

9. Many successful entrepreneurs had previous work experience in the same types of business they started.

10. Many successful entrepreneurs developed their businesses part-time before quitting their paying jobs.

11. Entrepreneurs are *doers*.

12. Entrepreneurs test an idea—they do trials.

13. Entrepreneurs learn and iterate, tinker and get better.

14. Entrepreneurs listen to customers.

15. Entrepreneurs constantly get better and improve their products or services.

Chapter Two

Businesses generally fail for 8 fundamental reasons:

1. People choose a bad business opportunity.
2. People try to sell to the wrong customers.
3. People try to sell the wrong products or services.
4. People price their products improperly.
5. People overestimate the number and the speed at which people will buy.
6. People cannot manage the business so as to consistently produce high quality products on time at a profit.
7. Employee problems.
8. People cannot scale their businesses to accommodate customer demand.

Chapter Three

1. Business ideas are like sand at the beach—plentiful, but there are few new or unique business ideas.
2. Not every business *idea* will make a good business *opportunity*.
3. Your idea needs to "pencil"—that is, make economic sense.
4. The key "pencil" drivers are:
   - The amount of money you need to make
   - Net profit margin
   - Customer conversion rate
   - Customer traffic volume
   - Speed of sales
   - Customer buying frequency
   - Burn rate and staying power—how much time (money) can you invest until you make a profit?

5. Remember the 7 Ws:
   - **W**hat can I sell?
   - To **W**hom can I sell?
   - **W**hy will customers buy from me?
   - At **W**hat price?
   - **W**hat are my costs?
   - **W**hen will customers buy?
   - **W**hat will the competition do?

6. Common mistakes business starters make:
   - Overestimating the number of customer sales
   - Overestimating how fast people will buy
   - Underestimating their costs
   - Underestimating the competition

7. Owning a low margin business means:
   - You need a lot of customers.
   - Customers need to buy frequently.
   - You will have to operate very efficiently.
   - Your room for financial mistakes or errors will be small.
   - Volume of customer traffic, customer conversion rates, and knowing the competition is very important.

8. Owning a higher margin business generally means:
   - You need fewer customers.
   - Your customers probably will not be frequent buyers.
   - You will need to consistently generate new customer prospects.
   - Customer conversion rates could be low.
   - You need a constant flow of good customer prospects.

9. Your estimated weekly costs help you predict your *burn rate*: the speed at which you will burn through your money. Burn rate tells you how long you can stay in business until you hit break-even.

10. *Break-even* is the point at which your weekly incoming cash equals your costs going out.

"The sole purpose of business is to serve customers."

—*Peter Drucker*

"If you do not make a profit in your business, you are a charity—a not-for-profit."

—*Ed Hess*

Chapter Four

1. Your company's likelihood for success is directly tied to identifying your prospects' most important needs and wants and then providing a solution that best meets their objectives.

2. Because not all prospects are equally as likely to buy your product or service, it's important that you determine which specific prospects are most interested in buying your product or service and what's different about them from the rest of the market.

   Prospects who are the most likely to buy your product or service are your target market.

3. The benefits of identifying targeted prospects include marketing and advertising savings, more enhanced product or service design, and increased sales.

4. Doing your homework is critical to your success.

5. Talk to people—learn firsthand people's needs/wants.

6. Constantly survey prospects, customers, and the competition.

7. Know your competitors' strengths and weaknesses so that you can take advantage of their limitations and better serve your targeted customers.

8. Your goal is to spend your time on high-probability prospects.

9. You have limited time and money. Do your research, focus, and be disciplined.

Chapter Five

1. Customers buy solutions, so you must constantly assess what customers really want or need and make sure you give them that—*not* what you think they need nor more than they need because they will not want to pay for anything they do not need.

2. The goal is to deliver the most value to your customer at a cost that is both affordable for your customer and profitable for you.

3. Avoid the Winner's Curse—overconfidence and complacency.

4. The competitive advantage you are seeking is to offer more value at an affordable price and do it defect-free, on time, and with good service every time.

5. Don't fall in love with your product or service—that is the job of your customers.

6. Go to market as fast as possible—learn from your customers.

7. Get customer references as soon as you can—they will help you make more sales.

8. Product benefits are necessities. Product features are options.

9. The Value Proposition Ratio is Value = Benefits ÷ Costs.

10. Value is what the customer perceives it to be—not what you think it is.

11. Your "reason for being" is your essence, your differentiator, and what your business stands for in the minds of customers.

12. Low innovation product design is less risky than developing a totally new product.

13. Remember you have to be able to build or produce your product reliably and 99% defect-free, on time, and at a profit.

14. Develop a prototype and get in the market quickly and learn from your customers. Test and learn and adapt and improve. Constant improvement is key.

Chapter Six

1. Price impacts your volume of sales and your profit.
2. Profit = Sales Price − Costs
3. There are two types of costs: fixed and variable.
4. Variable costs vary with your volume of product sold.
5. Review your costs monthly.
6. Price also determines your break-even volume—the amount you need to sell to earn enough profit to cover your costs.
7. Cost plus pricing and competitive pricing are two good pricing strategies.
8. You may have to offer guarantees or payment terms to certain customers.
9. Remember—to you, cash is king.

Chapter Seven

1. Customer inertia is real and serious.
2. To make a sale, you need to overcome obstacles to sale.
3. You cannot overcome what you do not understand. You have to ask questions and listen.
4. The sale starts when you understand the reasons why the prospect does not want to buy.
5. There are 9 common reasons people do not buy.
6. There are 7 techniques to get people to try your product.
7. Selling is like fishing—find the right hook.
8. Understand the customer timeline to buy.
9. Reward customer referrals and loyalty.

Chapter Eight

1. Management is the daily focus on producing high-quality products on time that meet customer needs, and it is the coordination of supplies, parts, processes, and people to get that desired result.

2. Every business has a value chain that should focus on the parts of the business you need to manage.

3. You need to develop value chain as well as supply chain and manufacturing chain flow charts.

4. Management's goal is to get the same high-quality result 99% of the time.

5. Management achieves 99% high-quality results through processes— drilling each job down to each step needed to complete it well.

6. Employees not only have to learn the job but also have to get better and faster; they have to constantly improve.

7. Good managers manage daily by objectives—the prioritized to-dos.

8. Good managers teach at least 15 minutes everyday to all employees the key objectives, the "have-to-dos" to be successful and the "cannot-dos."

9. Managing by exception is how you focus on the mistakes and problems.

10. Mistakes are a given. The key is to find them out quickly and fix them before they become big mistakes.

11. KISS: Keep It Simple, Stupid.

12. Learn to communicate clearly, concisely, and compellingly.

13. Constant improvement is far more important than doing it right the first time.

14. Structure becomes necessary when you have more than seven employees.

15. Measuring employees' performance is critical.

16. Measure the right things. Measure behaviors that create the right results.

17. Measure frequently and give results to all employees.

18. Reward what you measure.

19. Make work fun; make work a game to learn.

20. Create a constant improvement business, a high-performance environment.

21. High-performance environments are positive, energetic places to work and are based on the Golden Rule.

22. You need the committed hearts and minds of your employees to make money.

Chapter Nine

1. Employees are people, too. They want the same exact things you want—dignity, respect, and the opportunity to be all they can be.

2. Hire for *fit*; focus on values and character. You can teach skills—you cannot teach character and drive.

3. Become good at hiring. Hire only after a thorough investigation and a probationary period. Hire people with a track record of success.

4. Hire employees who are like your customers. They will understand and relate to your customers better.

5. Play to people's strengths. You do not have enough time to fix people's weaknesses.

6. Be clear about what the job is. Be truthful and manage expectations.

7. Teach—Teach—Teach.

8. Inform your employees often what behaviors are *not* tolerated. Give daily/weekly feedback and keep records.

9. Be fair, consistent, and honest. Lead by example.

10. Ask your employees monthly if they are happy. If they aren't, why not? Happy employees result in happy customers. How you treat your employees is the critical determination of whether they are happy and how they will perform.

11. Make work fun and meaningful, and when you can, always promote from within.

12. High-performance organizations create a "family."

13. Remember: Happy Employees + Happy Customers = You make money.

14. Take care of your people.

15. Manage yourself as thoroughly as you manage your employees. Mentally rehearse the day to come and mentally replay the previous day to see where you can make improvement.

Chapter Ten

1. Growth can be good or bad.

2. Growth creates people, quality, and financial issues.

3. Growth requires more controls and processes.

4. Growth requires the entrepreneur to become a manager.

5. Managing is different than doing.

6. Every financial area of your business (supplies, inventory, accounting, cash management, HR, and training employees) will need more process and controls.

7. Controls and processes have to be created real-time as you operate the business.

8. Growth will require you to upgrade your employees.

9. Growth will require you to manage customer concentration risk.

10. Growth will require more legal and insurance costs.

11. Growth will stretch you and will require you to operate differently.

12. Growth will require you to manage more proactively than reactively.

13. Growth will change your competition.

Bibliography and Resources[1]

Books

"Building a Company" Books

Bethune, Gordon. *From Worst to First*. New York: John Wiley, 1998.

The story of how Gordon Bethune took Continental Airlines from last place to first place. A good management, leadership, and execution book with lessons on how to keep focused on the customer. (ISBN 0-471-24835-5)

Cathy, S. Truett. *Eat Mor Chikin: Inspire More People*. Decatur, GA: Looking Glass Books, 2002.

The story of Truett and Jeannette Cathy's journey from one restaurant to building a restaurant empire based on values, character, and spirituality. All Chick-fil-A stores are closed on Sundays, and the Cathy family's success has been passed on to the second generation. (ISBN 1-929619-08-1)

Chouinard, Yvon. *Let My People Go Surfing*. New York: Penguin Books, 2005.

This is the story of Patagonia and how a successful business crashed and rescued itself. (ISBN 0-1430-37838)

Dell, Michael with Catherine Fredman. *Direct from Dell*. New York: HarperBusiness, 1999.

From dorm room to transforming and dominating an industry, the Michael Dell story is the story of the creation of a new logistics-supply chain model, which has made just-in-time manufacturing logistics a business necessity. (ISBN 0-88730-914-3)

[1]Adapted from Hess, Edward D. *The Successful Family Business*. Westport, CT: Praeger Publishers, 2006. (ISBN 0-275-98887-2)

Goetz, Charles F., and Michael E. Axelrod. *The Great Entrepreneurial Divide—The Winning Tactics of Successful Entrepreneurs and Why Everyone Else Fails!* Georgia: Rathskeller Press, 2007.

This book explores what successful entrepreneurs do differently than the less successful entrepreneurs and how the reader can benefit from it. New entrepreneurial concepts are introduced that will help first-time entrepreneurs and serial entrepreneurs increase their likelihood of success. (ISBN 978-0-9799745-0-2)

Hess, Edward D. *The Road to Organic Growth*. New York: McGraw-Hill, 2007.

This book describes how great growth companies continuously improve, engage their employees, and build a growth culture. The lessons are good for businesses of all sizes. (ISBN 007147525-7)

Marcus, Bernie, and Arthur Blank with Bob Andelman. *Built from Scratch*. New York: Times Business, 1999.

The story of how two fired friends rebounded to create and build the highly successful Home Depot Company. Like many other successful entrepreneurs—Sam Walton, Ross Perot, Howard Schultz—Marcus and Blank saw an opportunity in their industry their employer did not see. And the result was that they all did it their way. (ISBN 0-8129-3058-4)

Meyer, Danny. *Setting the Table*. New York: HarperCollins, 2006.

A great read by a consummate, caring, people-centric entrepreneur whose passion permeates the book. Uplifting and informative. (ISBN 0-06-074275-5)

O'Reilly, Charles A. *Hidden Value*. Boston: HBS Press, 2000.

Stanford University's answer to "how great companies achieve extraordinary results with ordinary people," focusing on eight companies including Southwest Airlines, the Men's Warehouse, the SAS Institute, and others. (ISBN 0-87584-898-2)

Reiss, Bob, with Jeffrey L. Cruikshank. *Low Risk, High Reward: Starting and Growing Your Business with Minimal Risk*. New York: Free Press, 2000.

This book is used by Charlie in his introductory-level entrepreneurship course. *Low Risk, High Reward* does an exceptional job in focusing first-time entrepreneurs on understanding the importance of risk and reward as it relates to being a successful entrepreneur.

Roddick, Anita. *Body and Soul*. New York: Crown, 1991.

The remarkable story of how a non-business housewife opens a shop to support herself and her children while her husband leaves England to accomplish his life's goal of riding a horse across South America. From one shop to a corporate empire, to an empire lost and regained, to a noted leader of corporate sustainability, fair trade, and corporate ethics. (ISBN 0-517-88134-0)

Schultz, Howard, and Dori Jones Yang. *Pour Your Heart Into It*. New York: Hyperion, 1997.

The Starbucks story from the Projects of The Bronx to the creation of a company that continues to grow. The role of values, the ground-breaking benefits given to employees, and how Howard Schultz kept his promise not to treat his employees like his father was treated. A great read about perseverance, character, and good mentors. (ISBN 0-7868-6397-8)

Swofford, Stan. *Rhino Tough*. Down Home Press, 2006.

A fascinating book about Ed's friend, Billy Prim, who built Blue Rhino, his successes and near failure and rebound. Reads like a novel. This stuff happens. (ISBN 0-9767829-1-X)

Walton, Sam, with John Huey. *Sam Walton, Made In America*. New York: Bantam Books, 1992.

Sam Walton's autobiography. The story of how he learned from his mother to excel and to be driven to succeed and the role of his wife and daughter in influencing Wal-Mart policies. His business model and the creation of a "family" atmosphere with his employees are crucial to understanding what Wal-Mart was under Sam Walton. (ISBN 0-553-56283-5)

Business Strategy Books

D'Aveni, Richard A. *Hypercompetition.* New York: Free Press, 1994.

Ed's friend, Professor Rich D'Aveni, of the Amos Tuck School at Dartmouth, puts forth a hyper-competition model for our fast-paced, changing, volatile, global world. The importance of this book is its emphasis that one's strategy should not be static, but rather one's strategy is an iterative, evolving proactive response to industry changes and competitor thrusts and countermoves. A dynamic approach to business strategy. (ISBN 0029069386)

Hargadon, Andrew. *How Breakthroughs Happen: The Surprising Truth About How Companies Innovate.* Boston: HBS Press, 2003.

A counter-intuitive book that gives hope to us normal people that most businesses can innovate without hiring geniuses and research types. The surprising truth of Andy's research is that most innovation occurs because people take ideas, products, and services from one domain to another— they move ideas across industries. (ISBN 1-57851-904-7)

Joyce, William, and Nitin Nohria. *What Really Works: The 4+2 Formula for Sustained Business Success.* New York: HarperCollins, 2003.

What makes successful companies successful? That is the million dollar question. Three professors likewise set out to crack the DNA of success and came away with their 4+2 model. They share what they learned about strategy, execution, culture, organization plus talent, leadership, innovation, and mergers. (ISBN 0-06-051278-4)

Mintzberg, Henry, Bruce Ahlstrand, and Joseph Lampel. *Strategy Safari: A Guided Tour Through the Wilds of Strategic Management.* New York: Free Press, 1998.

Professor Mintzberg is a brilliant strategist. Ed hired him once to teach strategy to a global group of my executives and he was spell-binding. This book is a great overview of the ten competing schools of strategy with a summary of each model. These models take either an inside-out viewpoint or an outside-in-viewpoint. A wonderful, thought-provoking read. (ISBN 0-13-695677-7)

Porter, Michael E. *Competitive Strategy*. New York: Free Press, 1980.

If you only ever read one book on strategy, this should be it. Professor Porter of the Harvard Business Schools gives you the methodology to analyze your industry and your competitors. His "5 Forces" are used by every company strategist we know, and he clearly states that every business needs to adopt one of two strategies: A volume low-cost producer or a niche differentiator. Professor Porter taught us the overriding importance of switching costs—the difficulty in convincing customers to change. (ISBN 0-02-025360-8)

Entrepreneurship Books

Drucker, Peter F., *Innovation and Entrepreneurship*. New York: Harper & Row, 1985.

The best management thinker of recent time. (ISBN 0-06-085113-9)

Gerber, Michael E. *The E-Myth Revisited: Why Most Small Businesses Don't Work and What to Do About It*. New York: HarperBusiness, 1995.

This book discusses why most small businesses fail and the difficulty of entrepreneurs moving from being a doer to a manager of others. (ISBN 0-88730-728-0)

Kuratko, Donald F., and Harold P. Welsch. *Strategic Entrepreneurial Growth*. Fort Worth: Harcourt College Publishers, 2001.

A very good business school textbook on entrepreneurship, building a business, and managing a business. Includes topics of innovation, globalization, and family business succession. (ISBN 0-03-031936-6)

McGrath, Rita Gunther, and Ian C. MacMillan. *The Entrepreneurial Mindset*. Boston: HBS Press, 2000.

The best book for learning entrepreneurial methodologies or analytical frameworks. The tools are useful no matter what the stage of your business. Discovery-driven planning, real options thinking, consumption chains, and product attribute maps are examples of useful tools. Ed uses this book in teaching executive education to corporate leaders. (ISBN 0-87584-834-6)

Timmons, Jeffrey A. *New Venture Creation: Entrepreneurship for the 21ˢᵗ Century*. 6ᵗʰ ed. Boston: McGraw-Hill/Irwin, 2004.

The best entrepreneurship book Ed has found and which he used in his Emory Entrepreneurship Course. From opportunity recognition, to screening opportunities, to financing growth, to managing rapid growth, to exiting a business—this book contains great checklists and processes for every business manager. (ISBN 0-256-11548-6)

Family Business Books

Aronoff, Craig E., Joseph H. Astrachan, and John L. Ward. *Developing Family Business Policies: Your Guide to the Future*. Marietta, GA: Family Enterprise Publishers, 1998.

A good checklist of family business policies. (ISBN 1-891652-01-X)

Gersick, Kelin E., John A. Davis, Marion McCollom Hampton, and Iva Lansberg. *Generation to Generation: Life Cycles of the Family Business*. Boston: HBS Press, 1997.

Two academics and two consultants collaborate to put forth a model for how family businesses evolve and the different roles family members can play as family members, employees, and owners. (ISBN 0-87584-555-4)

Hess, Edward D. *The Successful Family Business: A Proactive Plan for Managing the Family and the Business*. Westport, CT: Praeger Publishers, 2006.

Ed's practical guide to common family issues that arise in a family business. (ISBN 0-275-98887-2)

Lansberg, Ivan. *Succeeding Generations: Realizing the Dream of Families in Business*. Boston: HBS Press, 1999.

This book focuses on succession and the complex issues involved in managing a succession. A good but long read on marshalling a family's dream, the selection process, the governance issues, and about letting go. (ISBN 0-87584-742-0)

Ward, John L. *Keeping the Family Business Healthy*. Business Owner Resources, 1997.

Fundamentally, a strategy book for managing and perpetuating a family business. A good basic primer. (ISBN 1-55542-026-5)

Ward, John L. *Perpetuating the Family Business*. New York: Palgrave Macmillan, 2004.

This, in my opinion, is John Ward's best book—what he has learned in his 25 years teaching, researching, and consulting. This book will reinforce many of the lessons you learned in Ed's book. (ISBN 1-4039-3397-9)

Finance, Accounting, and Measurement Books

Bruner, Robert F. *Deals From Hell: M&A Lessons that Rise Above the Ashes*. Hoboken, NJ: Wiley, 2005.

Bob Bruner is the dean at the University of Virginia Darden School of Business and is one of the leading authorities on mergers. Do they work? Under what conditions? And what are the common pitfalls? A must-read for anyone thinking of merging their business or selling for stock. (ISBN 978-0-471-39595-9)

Copeland, Thomas E., Tim Koller, and Jack Murrin. *Valuation: Measuring and Managing the Value of Companies*. 2nd ed. New York: Wiley, 1994.

The bible of valuation written by three McKinsey & Company professionals. This book should answer your questions on discounted cash flow projections, EBITDA versus accounting net income, the real cost of financing or capital, values-based management, and finding the value drivers of your business. (ISBN 0-471-36190-9)

Fridson, Martin, and Fernando Alvarez. *Financial Statement Analysis: A Practitioner's Guide*. 3rd ed. New York: John Wiley & Sons, 2002.

An outstanding book for those with a basic understanding of accounting. A compendium of common issues in understanding securities offerings and evaluating competitors' or targets' financial statements. The ways numbers can be massaged or manipulated. (ISBN 0-471-40915-4)

Kaplan, Robert S., and David P. Norton. *The Balanced Scorecard: Translating Strategy into Action*. Boston: HBS Press, 1996.

How do you measure results? How do you measure employee or business unit results? Many businesses today utilize some form of balanced scorecard to link measurements and strategy and to achieve strategic alignment of their different business units, departments, or functions. This book makes it possible for every business, regardless of size, to measure better and hold people accountable. (ISBN 0-87584-651-3)

Schilit, Howard. *Financial Shenanigans: How to Detect Accounting Gimmicks and Fraud in Financial Reports*. 2nd ed. New York: McGraw-Hill, 2002.

From the pioneer of accounting sleuthdom, the common accounting gimmicks and ways to manipulate the financial picture of a company. Use this checklist to evaluate the financial statements of the business you may want to buy. (ISBN 0-07-138626-2)

Stern, Joel M. and Donald H. Chew, editors. *The Revolution in Corporate Finance*. 2nd ed. Cambridge, MA: Blackwell Finance, 1992.

A compendium of fine articles on the topics of capital budgeting, cost of capital, capital structures, raising capital, interest rate swaps, and spin-offs, carve-outs, and divestitures. (ISBN 0-631-18554-2)

Leadership Books

Badaracco, Joseph. *Leading Quietly*. Boston: HBS Press, 2002.

Joe Badaracco is a wonderful, humble leader and professor at Harvard Business School. He graciously helped Ed when he was beginning his teaching career with no motivation other than kindness. He, in this book, dispels the myths of leadership and asserts that leadership is patient, careful, and incremental. He lays out a framework or template for leadership analysis and action. (ISBN 1-57851-487-8)

Behar, Howard. *It's Not About the Coffee*. Portfolio, 2007.

A good book on leadership and people-centric policies at Starbucks. (ISBN 9781591841920)

Bennis, Warren G. and Robert J. Thomas. *Geeks & Geezers*. Boston: HBS Press, 2002.

The authors look at the role of adversity in a leader's life. They correctly focus on the fact that in extremely difficult times, character, confidence, and values are solidified and that adversity prepares one to deal with life's challenges. (ISBN 1-57851-582-3)

George, Bill. *Authentic Leadership*. San Francisco: Jossey-Bass, 2003.

Bill George is the former chairman and CEO of Medtronic. His book is an illuminating story about the authentic leadership model. He focuses on purposes, values, and self-discipline and gives one hope in this era of corporate scandals that one can lead with values and morals and create shareholder value, too. (ISBN 0-7879-6913-3)

Gergen, David R. *Eyewitness to Power*. New York: Simon & Schuster, 2000.

The subtitle of David Gergen's book is *The Essence of Leadership: Nixon to Clinton*, and he does not disappoint. A thoughtful work focusing on style, checks, and balances, character, and power. The pros and cons of each president's leadership are here for all to learn from. (ISBN 0-684-82663-1)

Goleman, Daniel, Richard E. Boyatzis, and Annie McKee. *Primal Leadership: Realizing the Power of Emotional Intelligence*. Boston: HBS Press, 2002.

Goleman and his colleagues at Rutgers and Case Western University have put the leadership onus right back where it belongs—on you. Our effectiveness as leaders is dependent on our emotional intelligence. Our ability to manage our emotions, understand others' motions, and to relate and connect to people emotionally. A must-read for every male. (ISBN 1-57851-486-X)

Greenleaf, Robert K. *Servant Leadership*. New York: Paulist Press, 2002.

Robert Greenleaf, a former AT&T executive, in 1977 espoused that service to others was the essence of leadership. Servant leadership is growing in popularity and is also known as values-based leadership. (ISBN 0-8091-0554-3)

Books on Lessons to Learn from Bad Leadership

Eichenwald, Kurt. *Conspiracy of Fools: A True Story*. New York: Broadway Books, 2005.

A spell-binding account of the inner working of Enron from a corporate finance viewpoint primarily. Reads like a mystery thriller. It tells the story of when management loses touch with the details, condones inappropriate behavior, and compensates people for the wrong results. Wall Street's role in this disaster is not pretty. And Arthur Andersen's overriding of its quality control people in order to satisfy Enron is shameful. (ISBN 0-7679-1178-4)

McLean, Bethany, and Peter Elkind. *The Smartest Guys in the Room: The Amazing Rise and Scandalous Fall of Enron*. New York: Portfolio, 2003.

The story of the Enron Company—its culture, value, and leadership. How the greed of the 1990s impacted the ability of accountants, lawyers, and Wall Street to render their duties to the investing public. The story of arrogance, hubris, greed without values, and form over substance. How smart, "normal" people got caught up in peer pressure and lost their anchors or moral compasses for what is right and wrong. (ISBN 1-59184-008-2)

Stewart, James B. *Disney War*. New York: Simon & Schuster, 2005.

The excruciating details of an autocratic, insecure CEO who packed his board with those beholden to him. The pettiness, the duplicity, and the failure of core values are mind-boggling. The story is like a soap opera, and much can be learned about the CEO's decision-making processes. (ISBN 0-684-80993-1)

Management Books

Bossidy, Larry, and Ram Charan with Charles Burck. *Execution: The Discipline of Getting Things Done*. New York: Crown Business, 2002.

Bossidy and Charan refocused U.S. business leadership on the key role of execution. The best strategy in the world is not worth much if you cannot execute it. Bossidy's mantra is a culture of critical inquiry that produces reality for management. His views on constructive debate, measurement, and rewards are spot on. He sets forth the GE model of aligning strategy and action. (ISBN 0-609-61057-0)

Buckingham, Marcus, and Curt Coffman. *First, Break All the Rules*. New York: Simon and Schuster, 1999.

This book would have sold even more copies with a representative title. Ed uses it in his classes. It is the best book to teach you how to manage people—how to communicate, set objectives, and hold people accountable, and it is a primer for managing people best practices—based on years of research by Gallup. (ISBN 0-684-85285-1)

Collins, James C. *Good to Great*. New York: HarperBusiness, 2001.

Jim Collins produced the best-selling business book since *Search For Excellence*. (ISBN 0-06-662099-6)

Finkelstein, Sydney. *Why Smart Executives Fail and What You Can Learn from Their Mistakes*. New York: Portfolio, 2003.

Professor Finkelstein's book is a welcomed addition. His research shows that most major business failures occur in big transactions: mergers, change initiatives, new competition, and they occur because of leadership's arrogance, hubris, insularity, and from flawed cognition—the failure to see and process reality. If you are successful, a must-read to stay successful. (ISBN 1-59184-010-4)

Hamel, Gary. *The Future of Management*. Boston: HBS Press, 2007.

A thought-provoking read on how to build a modern business where all stakeholders win. (ISBN 1-4221-0250-5)

Magretta, Joan. *What Management Is*. New York: Free Press, 2002.

This book brings all of us back to the basics of what is management. Anytime you get caught up in either management hype or think you have figured the management game out—you should pull this book off the shelf and read it. (ISBN 0-7432-0318-6)

Sullivan, Gordon R., and Michael V. Harper. *Hope Is Not a Method*. New York: Broadway Books, 1997.

If you need to change something major in your business, read this book about the U.S. Army's massive change initiative in the early 1990s. One of the best books on the execution of change. (ISBN 0-7679-0060-4)

Marketing and Sales Books

Bedbury, Scott with Stephen Fenichell. *A New Brand World: 8 Principles for Achieving Brand Leadership in the 21st Century*. New York: Viking, 2002.

From 1995 to 1998 Scott Bedbury was senior vice president of marketing at Starbucks and prior to that, the head of advertising at Nike. Need I say more? A thought-provoking book on the power of brand—what your company represents. Just maybe your most important product is your brand. (ISBN 0-670-03076-7)

Heskitt, James L., W. Earl Sasser, and Leonard A. Schlesinger. *The Service Profit Chain*. New York: Free Press, 1997.

Using Southwest Airlines, Ritz-Carlton, Taco Bell, and others, these three Harvard Business School professors irrefutably establish the link between employee satisfaction and customer satisfaction and loyalty and profits. This book from the logistics and marketing worlds confirms the role of values, people-centric cultures, and employee satisfaction in driving business results. (ISBN 0-684-83256-9)

Kotler, Philip. *Kotler on Marketing*. New York: Free Press, 1999.

Northwestern University's dean of marketing with over 15 books to his credit. He views marketing as a competitive advantage and a disciplined strategy. Thought-provoking and it will change your view. (ISBN 0-68-85033-8)

Sheth, Jagdish N., and Rajendra S. Sisodia. *The Rule of Three: Surviving and Thriving in Competitive Markets*. New York: Free Press, 2002.

Ed's friend, Jag Sheth, has produced the theory that in every industry, three companies will dominate a market. The authors give hope to small firms who specialize and who do not get too big to become a target of the Big 3. (ISBN 0-7432-0560-X)

Articles

The most consistent source of high-quality business articles written for the business person is the *Harvard Business Review*. Some favorites follow:

Collins, Jim, "Level 5 Leadership: The Triumph of Humility and Fierce Resolve," *HBR*, January 2001, 66–76.

Good to Great, the # 1 best selling business book of the last ten years busted the myth about leaders of great businesses. No, they are generally not charismatic larger-than-life heroes. They are humble, passionately-focused people.

Collis and Montgomery, "Creating Corporate Advantage," *HBR*, May/June 1998, 70–83.

How do you align your strategy, structure, control processes, and human resources to maximize your chances of success? Three different models are discussed based on Tyco, Sharp Electronics, and Newell Rubbermaid.

Couter, Diane L., "Sense and Reliability—A Conversation with Celebrated Psychologist Karl E. Werck," *HBR*, April 2003, 84–90.

Ed heard Karl Werck talk in February 2005 at one of my conferences about high reliability organizations, and in 30 minutes he added a whole new dimension to his thought process. Successful organizations not only reward values they cherish, they also focus on non-desired behaviors. This article discusses high reliability organizations like air traffic controller teams, fire fighters, and emergency room personnel.

Drucker, Peter F., "Managing Oneself," *HBR*, March/April 1999, 64–74.

A wonderful article about the toughest management job in the world—managing yourself. Most people do not spend the time to assess themselves and put themselves into position to play to their strengths. Drucker's "mirror" test is a good one for any leader, parent, or partner.

Magretta, Joan, "Governing the Family-Owned Enterprise: An Interview with Finland's Krister Ahlstrom," *HBR*, Jan-Feb 1998, 112–123.

A thought-provoking interview with the non-family CEO of a large multi-generational family business dealing with issues of governance, the different roles family members play, how to keep the family connected to the business, the roles of Family Councils, and a Family Values Statement.

Miller, Warren D., "Siblings and Succession in the Family Business," *HBR* Jan-Feb 1998, 22–36.

Three family members vying to be the successor CEO is the recipe for disaster. This Harvard case study is illustrative of the problems of having too many family members working in the business. Four outside experts present their advice. Some practical, some not.

Pearson, Andrall E., "Tough-Minded Ways to Get Innovative," *HBR*, August 2002, 117–124.

The former President of Pepsi Co. has more good advice in these seven pages than most books have. He demystifies innovation and growth.

Porter, Lorsch, Norhia, "Seven Surprises for New CEOs," *HBR*, October 2004, 62–72.

A good article for new CEOs of both public and private companies—and yes, family businesses. Generally, CEOs overestimate how fast and how much they can impact an organization. Lessons to be learned—do not think it is about you, and do not lose touch with the line employees and customers.

Rogers, Holland, and Haas, "Value Acceleration: Lessons from Private Equity Masters," *HBR*, June 2002, 94–101.

Private equity firms have an expertise in buying firms, operating them for a few years, and either doing an IPO or selling the business at a very good return. Why can these financial engineers run businesses better than management? The authors of the consulting firm, Bain & Company, studied 2,000 private equity transactions and came away with four key managerial principles that can apply to your business, too.

Slywotzky, Adrian J., and Richard Wise, "The Growth Crisis and How to Escape It," *HBR*, July 2002, 72–83.

In the decade of the 1990s, less than 10% of the public companies grew their revenues 10% or more in eight or more years. Consistent top-line growth is hard. What works? Geographical expansion, acquisitions, price increases, innovation? Their answer lies in your existing customer relationships.

Special Issue: "Inside the Mind of the Leader," *HBR*, January 2004.

Buy this whole journal. It contains good articles by Warren Bennis (*Geeks and Geezers*), Daniel Goleman (*Primal Leadership*), Colleen Barrett of Southwest Airlines, and David Gergen.

Ed uses "When Followers Become Toxic" by Lynn R. Offerman in his leadership classes to discuss "Yes People" and "Corporate Suck-Ups."

Information Portals

1. *Entreworld.org* is the information portal of the Kauffman Foundation. Its content is broken down into three parts: starting your business, growing your business, and supporting entrepreneurship. Starting your business has nine subtitles:

   - You, the Entrepreneur
   - Market Evaluation
   - Product/Service Development
   - The Right People
   - Finances
   - Marketing and Sales
   - Legal and Taxes
   - Technology
   - Special Interest Groups

   Under each subtitle are 3 to 7 content areas.

   Likewise, growing your business has nine subtitles with 3 to 10 content areas. Critical new ones are accessing capital and growth strategies.

   The Entrepreneur Search Engine has a wealth of information listed under: Academic Materials, Organizations, Publications, Research, Center for Entrepreneurship, Distance Learning, and Family Business.

   The Family Business section lists 32 Family Business Centers at universities with links to their sites.

2. *Fambiz.com* is the family business portal of Northeastern University. It has a good article search feature.

3. *Ffi.org*, Family Firm Institute, is a consultant organization that publishes *The Family Business Review*.

4. www.kennesaw.edu/fec (Cox Family Enterprise Center) is run by Ed's friend, Joe Astraclan. He is the editor of *The Family Business Review* and Cox published family business cases.

5. www.knowledge.wharton.upenn.edu is a good, free information source from top-ranked Wharton Graduate Business School.

6. www.gsb.stanford.edu is the Stanford Knowledgebase and a good, free information source about business thought leadership. Stanford's Executive Education site has an outstanding catalog of speeches on CDE for reasonable prices.

Author's Commentaries

These commentaries were written by Ed Hess for private company CEOs and owners, and the content is explained in the titles. These commentaries can be found on his web site: www.EDHLTD.com.

"10 Keys to Raising Growth Capital," *The Catalyst*, April 2004.

"Are Your Employees a Means to Your End?" *The Catalyst*, May 2004.

"Blocking and Tackling," *The Catalyst*, December 2003.

"Corporate Social Responsibility: The Value of Business Stewardship," *The Catalyst*, October 2004.

"Do You Have a Broken Arrow Plan?" *The Catalyst*, August 2003.

"Entrepreneurial Leadership: Why Should Anyone Follow You?" *The Catalyst*, June 2003

"Entrepreneurs: Reality vs. Myth," *The Catalyst*, July 2004.

"Going Public to Get Rich: Reality Therapy," *The Catalyst*, April 2003.

"Independent Directors: Private Companies Need Them," *The Catalyst*, March 2003.

"Managing Execution," *The Catalyst*, January 2003.

"Managing the Family Business: The Golden Goose and the Sandbox," *The Catalyst*, May 2003.

"Managing VUCA," *The Catalyst*, June 2004.

"Rapid Growth: Be Careful What You Ask For," *The Catalyst*, July 2003.

"The Family Business Succession: The Duality Principle," *The Catalyst*, February 2004.

"The Family Business: The Unintended Consequences of Gifts of Stock," *The Catalyst*, January 2004.

"The 'Perfect' Investment," *The Catalyst*, September 2004.

"The Silver Bullet of Leadership," *The Catalyst*, November 2004.

"What Do Good Leaders Actually Do? (Part I)," *The Catalyst*, September 2003.

"What Do Good Leaders Actually Do? (Part II)," *The Catalyst*, November 2003.

"What Is the Meaning of Business?" *The Catalyst*, October 2003.

"When Should Your Business Stop Growing," *The Catalyst*, March 2004.

"Why Successful Companies Often Fail," *The Catalyst*, February 2003.

Index

A–B

assembling (manufacturing) chain, defined, 101-102

benefits (of products), defined, 60
beta tests, defined, 70-71
Blanchard, Jimmy, 126
break-even, defined, 37
break-even formula, defined, 81-82
burn rate, defined, 37
business ideas
>business opportunities versus, 10-12
>evaluating
>>*children's clothing shop example, 30-32*
>>*cost estimations, 35-38*
>>*customer conversion ratio, 22*
>>*net profit margin, 22*
>>*net profit margin by business sector, 33-34*
>>*"penciling" ideas, 23-24*
>>*sandwich shop example, 24-30*
>>*7 Ws, 38*

business management. *See also* growth management
>defined, 98
>of employees, 114, 124-127
>by exceptions, 106-108

iteration, defined, 114
KISS principle, 108-109
manufacturing chain, defined, 101-102
measurements and rewards for employees, 110-113
>by objectives, 103-106
>rule of 3s, 109
>rule of 7s, 110
>start-up overload, 98
>supply chain, defined, 100
>value chain
>>*defined, 99-100*
>>*flow charting, 102-103*

business opportunities, business ideas versus, 10-12. *See also* evaluating business ideas
business success
>determining, 12
>rules of, 18-19

businesses, starting as employees, 94
buy-in of employees, 123

C

cash flow in growth management, 133-137
checklists, growth management, 135-136

children's clothing shop example
(evaluating business ideas), 30-32

competition
defining, 53
researching, 52, 54-56
sandwich shop example,
26-28

competitive advantage, determining, 66-68

competitive analysis, 55-56

competitive pricing, defined, 80

contingency plans, importance
of, 137

cost plus pricing, defined, 79-80

costs
defined, 5
estimating, 35-38, 78-80
competitive pricing, 80
cost plus pricing, 79-80

customer buying timeline, 92

Customer Conversion Rate, 14
children's clothing shop
example, 31
defined, 22
low profit margin versus high
profit margin, 32-33

customer feedback, importance of,
71-74

customer inertia, 14-15

customer loyalty programs, 94

customer referral programs, 94

customer segmentation, 12

customer service, importance of, 2

customer traffic, defined, 31

customer volume, determining,
28-30

customers
defined, 5, 42
diversification of, 142
high-probability prospects
defined, 43
finding, 44-46, 50-52
meeting needs of, 60
pricing factors regarding, 82-84
prospects, defined, 42
selecting, 12, 42-46, 50-52
at start-up, 94

D

daily improvement, 127

daily preparation, importance
of, 127

delivery channels, 12

design chart for products, 69-70

differentiators, defined, 66

diversification of customers, 142

Drucker, Peter, 2

E

employees
buy-in for job, 123
expectations of, 121
firing, 124, 142
growth management, 138

hiring
  for cultural fit, 121-122
  interviews and reference checks, 122
  probationary hiring, 123
  management of, 114, 124-127
  measurements and rewards, 110-113
  promoting, 125
  relationship with, 16-17
  starting businesses as, 94
  team environment for, 120, 126-127
  training, 124
  turnover, 121
  upgrading, 142
entrepreneurs
  common mistakes of, 10
  business opportunity selection, 10-12
  customer inertia, 14-15
  customer selection, 12
  employees, relationship with, 16-17
  growth management, 17-18
  poor execution, 15-16
  pricing, 13-14
  product selection, 12-13
  defined, 5
  paths to success of, 5
  skills needed by, 3-4
entrepreneurship, defined, 5

estimating costs, 35-38, 78-80
  competitive pricing, 80
  cost plus pricing, 79-80
evaluating business ideas
  children's clothing shop example, 30-32
  cost estimations, 35-38
  customer conversion ratio, 22
  net profit margin, 22
  by business sector, 33-34
  "penciling" ideas, 23-24
  sandwich shop example, 24-30
  7 Ws, 38
exceptions, management by, 106-108
Execution Process, defined, 102. *See also* running daily business

F

features (of products), defined, 60
feedback from customers, importance of, 71-74
financial controls, 137
financing growth management, 136-137
firing employees, 124, 142
fixed costs, defined, 78
flow charting value chains, 99, 102-103
fly fishing analogy (sales), 93
focus groups, defined, 44
fully loaded cost, defined, 79

G

Gates, Bill, 3
goals. *See* objectives
Google, competitive advantage, 67
growth management, 17-18, 132
    challenges of, 132-134
    checklists, 135-136
    contingency plans, 137
    customer diversification, 142
    employee issues, 138
    employees, upgrading, 142
    financial controls, 137
    financing, 136-137
    legal issues, 140-141
    priorities, setting, 134
    questions to ask, 142-144
    reports, 140
    small business networking, 141
    small business services, hiring, 139-140

H

high performance businesses, 17
high profit margin, customer conversion rates needed, 32-33
high-probability prospects
    defined, 43
    finding, 44-46, 50-52

hiring
    employees
        for cultural fit, 121-122
        interviews and reference checks, 122
        probationary hiring, 123
    small business services, 139-140
housing amenities example (Value Proposition Ratio), 62-66

I–J

ideas
    business opportunities versus, 10-12
    evaluating
        children's clothing shop example, 30-32
        cost estimations, 35-38
        customer conversion ratio, 22
        net profit margin, 22
        net profit margin by business sector, 33-34
        "penciling" ideas, 23-24
        sandwich shop example, 24-30
        7 Ws, 38
improvement, daily, 127
innovation, low versus high, 68
interviews, hiring employees, 122
iteration, defined, 114

K–L

KISS principle, 108-109

leadership, rules for, 126

legal issues in growth management, 140-141

low innovation, defined, 68

low profit margin, customer conversion rates needed, 32-33

M

mailing lists, buying, 51

management. *See also* growth management

    defined, 98

    of employees, 114, 124-127

    by exceptions, 106-108

    iteration, defined, 114

    KISS principle, 108-109

    manufacturing chain, defined, 101-102

    measurements and rewards for employees, 110-113

    by objectives, 103-106

    rule of 3s, 109

    rule of 7s, 110

    start-up overload, 98

    supply chain, defined, 100

    value chain

        defined, 99-100

        flow charting, 102-103

manufacturing chain, defined, 101-102

market surveys

    conducting, 45-46, 50-52

    defined, 44

    example of, 47-49

measurements (of employees), 110-113

mistakes, handling, 106-108

Monthly Payment Customers, defined, 82

N

net profit margin

    by business sector, 33-34

    customer conversion rates and, 32-33

    defined, 22

    determining customer volume, 28-30

    determining pricing, 25-26, 36

    researching competition, 26, 28

networking with small business owners, 141

O–P

objectives, management by, 103-106

obstacles to sales, overcoming, 88-91

opportunities, business ideas versus, 10-12. *See also* evaluating business ideas

overestimating number of customers, 14-15

pencil process, defined, 30

"penciling" business ideas, 23-24

people. *See* customers; employees

Perot, Ross, 3

Pfizer Pharmaceutical Company, competitive advantage, 67

positive cash flow, 12

preparation
    contingency plans, 137
    daily preparation, importance of, 127

pricing
    break-even formula, 81-82
    costs, estimating, 78-80
        competitive pricing, 80
        cost plus pricing, 79-80
    defined, 5
    determining, 25-26, 36
    factors in, 82-84
    setting, 13-14

primary research
    defined, 44
    market surveys
        conducting, 45-46, 50-52
        example of, 47-49

prioritization
    for growth management, 134
    of tasks, 103-106

probationary hiring, 123

processes
    checklists for, 135-136
    defined, 103

Product Differentiation Story (sales pitch), 12

products
    benefits, defined, 60
    break-even formula, 81-82
    competitive advantage, determining, 66-68
    customer feedback, importance of, 71, 73-74
    design chart for, 69-70
    features, defined, 60
    low innovation, defined, 68
    meeting customer needs, 60
    pricing, 13-14
    production considerations, 70
    prototypes, defined, 70-71
    selecting, 12-13
    Value Proposition Ratio
        defined, 61-62
        housing amenities example, 62-66

profit, defined, 5. *See also* net profit margin; your profit

promoting employees, 125

prospects
>defined, 42
>high-probability prospects
>>*defined, 43*
>>*finding, 44-46, 50-52*
prototypes, defined, 70-71
public companies, researching net profit margin of, 27

Q–R

qualified prospects, 12
quality, importance of, 132
quick sales, importance of, 93
"reason for being," determining, 66-68
recordkeeping, 138
reference checks, hiring employees, 122
reports, growth management, 140
researching
>competition, 26-28, 52-56
>customers. *See* high-probability prospects, finding
rewards (for employees), 110-113
Risk-Adverse Customers, defined, 83
rule of 3s, 109
rule of 7s, 110
running daily business, 15-16

S

sales. *See also* employees
>customer buying timeline, 92
>customer referral and loyalty programs, 94
>fly fishing analogy, 93
>listening, importance of, 92
>obstacles, overcoming, 88-91
>psychology of, 92
>quick sales, importance of, 93
>sense of urgency in, 88
sales pitch. *See* Product Differentiation Story (sales pitch)
sales price. *See* pricing
sandwich shop example (evaluating business ideas), 24-30
Schulte, Horst, 102
Schultz, Howard, 3
secondary research, defined, 44
selecting
>business opportunities, 10-12. *See also* evaluating business ideas
>customers, 12, 42-46, 50-52
>products, 12-13
services. *See* products
7 Ws
>evaluating business ideas, 38
>list of, 19
simplicity in management, 108-109

small business networking, 141

small business services, hiring, 139-140

start-up companies. *See* entrepreneurs

start-up overload, 98

start-up time, defined, 37

success
determining, 12
rules of, 18-19

supply chain, defined, 100

surveys. *See* market surveys

T

team environment for employees, 120, 126-127

3 Ws, list of, 74

Timing of Payment Customers, defined, 82

trade associations, defined, 45

training employees, 124

turnover of employees, 121

U–V

underestimating length of buying time, 14-15

upgrading employees, 142

value chain
defined, 99-100
flow charting, 102-103

Value Proposition Ratio
defined, 61-62
housing amenities example, 62-66

variable costs
defined, 78
examples of, 79

volume. *See* customer volume

W–Z

Wal-Mart, 122
competitive advantage, 67

Walton, Sam, 3, 122

your profit, defined, 5. *See also* profit